THE WARRIOR KINGS OF SAXON ENGLAND

THE

𝔚𝔞𝔯𝔯𝔦𝔬𝔯 𝔎𝔦𝔫𝔤𝔰

OF

𝔖𝔞𝔵𝔬𝔫 𝔈𝔫𝔤𝔩𝔞𝔫𝔡

RALPH WHITLOCK

DORSET PRESS
New York

This edition published by Dorset Press,
a division of Marboro Books Corporation.
1991 Dorset Press

ISBN 0-88029-673-9

Printed in the United States of America
M 9 8 7 6 5 4 3 2 1

Contents

With grateful acknowledgement to the unfailing and courteous help given by the staff of Yeovil Library.

Anglo-Saxon England, with the original home of the Anglo-Saxons inset

Introduction

The tradition of beginning English history-books with the reign of William the Conqueror and regarding anything that went before as a mere prologue has robbed the study of much of its excitement and interest. By the time the Normans appeared on the scene the country had enjoyed a period of civilization at least as long as from William the Conqueror to our own day, albeit with one or two violent interruptions. To these interludes belong the bold, bad days of our island story, comparable to the much-publicised and glamorised 'Winning of the West' in America.

Alfred, the one English monarch who has deservedly been accorded the title 'the Great', fought his battles nearly 200 years before the Battle of Hastings. His son, Edward, was one of the most effective monarchs who ever sat on the English throne. Yet, because of the convention that events before 1066 do not count, the Plantagenet Edward (1273 to 1307), is known as Edward I, and the Saxon Edward is identified as 'Edward the Elder' (which seems rather inappropriate for a man who became king when he was about thirty and died when he was no more than fifty-four). There was, as a matter of fact, a second Saxon king Edward, whose career was cut short by assassination when he was only fifteen and who should rightfully be labelled Edward II, and an Edward III, who was known as Edward the Confessor, thus making our Edward VIII (afterwards the Duke of Windsor) in reality Edward XI.

It is with the English, or Saxon, dynasty of which Alfred the Great, Edward the Elder and Edward the Martyr were members that this book is concerned. These kings resembled A. E. Houseman's army of mercenaries who

> In the day when heaven was falling,
> The hour when earth's foundations fled, . . .
> Their shoulders held the sky suspended;
> They stood, and earth's foundations stay.

1

Their motive, however, was not pay but patriotism. Matched against them was one of the most terrible challenges that Western civilization has ever had to face—a menace equal to that of Attila, Genghis Khan and Hitler. Theirs was literally a last-ditch stand (and with Alfred it really was a ditch—the ditch that surrounded the islet of Athelney, which was all that for a time remained of his kingdom). Behind them were no reserves, no place of retreat or refuge. They fought and conquered, or died where they stood.

Alfred's contribution has been best publicised, and rightly so, for his was the courage which first turned back the huge tide of heathendom, but he was not an isolated phenomenon. Before and after him came worthy kinsmen who fought the same enemy with similar energy. The West Saxon dynasty of which he was the oustanding member was, in fact, one of the most gifted, the most tenacious and the most remarkable in all history. As in the course of two centuries the barbarian armies launched assault after assault on our battered island, so the dynasty of Wessex produced leader after leader to meet the successive challenges. There have been many examples in history of the hour producing the man, but seldom if ever has a country produced such a succession of heroes.

Their story is the more remarkable because they were physically a rather sickly bunch. The malady which attacked Alfred and recurrently made his life a misery was evidently transmitted to his descendants. Few of them lived to be fifty, and short reigns were the rule rather than the exception. Edred, Alfred's grandson, is recorded (by William of Malmesbury) to have been intermittently sick and to have had 'so weak a digestion as to be unable to swallow more than the juices of the food he had masticated, to the great annoyance of his guests', in spite of which he proved a worthy and successful warrior in his reign of nine years. Edgar, who was crowned king of All England at Bath in 973, was almost a dwarf. William of Malmesbury relates a story of how one of his subject kings, Kinad, king of the Scots, remarked jocularly that 'it seemed extraordinary how so many provinces should be subject to such a sorry little fellow'. When this unwise comment was reported to Edgar, he lured Kinad into a wood and presenting him with a sword and retaining one for himself, invited him to prove his words. 'Nor shall you stir a foot till you try the matter with me,' he declared. Kinad thought it best to kneel and ask pardon, which was granted. And it was Edgar who in 959 required six tributary kings to row his boat in a ceremonial regatta on the river Dee at Chester.

The period in which this talented dynasty flourished is roughly 1000 years ago. To assist an understanding of the time-scale, therefore, it may be helpful to insert a '1' before each date as we encounter it. Egbert, who first brought the kingdom of Wessex to a position of supremacy in England, became king in 825. Edgar, after whom the dynasty suffered an eclipse, died in 925. The Saxon monarchy eventually came to an end in 1066. By transferring these dates into our present era, we arrive at a basic period of 1825 to 1975, with an extension to 2066. Living as we do in the 1970s, this exercise will help us to understand the perspective of our ancestors of the 970s as they looked back on earlier events. To them, Alfred's campaigns would be the equivalent of nineteenth-century wars to us, though in a largely illiterate age memories were probably more vivid and more detailed.

The sources of information about the period that have survived for 1000 years are naturally limited. The devastation caused by the barbarian invaders ensured that few records were kept, in the first place, and of those all but a very few perished. We have, however, several exceptionally valuable records of the times, perhaps the most important of all being *The Anglo-Saxon Chronicle*.

The *Chronicle* is a quite remarkable document in several respects, not least in that it was written in English rather than in monastic Latin. The earlier parts, up to the time of King Alfred, were probably based on seventh- or eighth-century documents, though we do not know what they were. Up to the ninth century the chronology is somewhat vague. In the course of the restoration of civilised values during the latter part of the reign of King Alfred, the king himself caused several complete copies to be made of the *Chronicle* to date and to be distributed to the chief ecclesiastical establishments, including Winchester, Canterbury, Peterborough and Worcester. Thereafter, scholars in each of these centres kept the record up-to-date until more than a hundred years after the Norman Conquest. From Alfred's time, too, it ceases to be a bare list of events and sometimes provides a wealth of detail, besides developing a definable literary style. There is very little to equal it for that period in any country in the world.

Supplementing the *Chronicle* for the vital years of Alfred's reign is a Latin work entitled (in its English translation) *The Annals of the Deeds of Alfred the Great*. It is ascribed to Asser, bishop of Sherborne and friend of King Alfred. Although some doubt has been cast on Asser's authorship, general opinion among scholars is in favour of it, and the book certainly seems to be contemporary or nearly so. Its account tallies accurately with that given in *The Anglo-Saxon Chronicle* but provides additional details.

A reliable historian who has also added much to our knowledge of the period, though he lived at a later date, was William of Malmesbury. As his name implies, William was a monk at Malmesbury Abbey. His latest work is dated 1142, demonstrating that he died after that year, and he was probably born between 1066 and the end of the century. As he mentions that he was of mixed Norman and English descent, he probably belonged to the first or second generation of the new, hybrid English who grew up after the Conquest. Of the 19 books he is known to have written the most important is *De Gestis Regum Anglorum* (*The History of the Kings of England*). In it he concentrated particularly on the period 751 to 1066. The first of these dates is that which marks the conclusion of Bede's *Ecclesiastical History of the English People*, another monumental work which deals in considerable detail with many events in the sixth, seventh and eighth centuries. William thus covers a gap for which our only other major source is *The Anglo-Saxon Chronicle*. Both he and Bede wrote in Latin; both were conscientious historians, making judicious use of their sources and refusing to be led astray into the byroads of fantasy and speculation.

Bede himself is concerned with a period prior to the one with which we are dealing but provides invaluable background information about Anglo-Saxon England.

Several British (Celtic) chronicles cover the period under review and add a little to our knowledge of it. *A History of the Kings of Britain* is usually attributed to an allegedly eighth- or ninth-century Welsh monk, Nennius, though the earliest surviving copies of the book are from the twelfth and thirteenth centuries. Another Celtic book, *De Excidio Britanniae* (*The Destruction of Britain*), attributed to the British monk Gildas, was evidently written before 547. For our purpose, therefore, both are useful only in supplying information about the prelude to the events with which we deal.

The *Welsh Annals* (*Annales Cambriae*) deal with the period of the conquest of Britain by the Anglo-Saxons, written of course from the British viewpoint, but the entries are laconic and scrappy. It is somewhat disconcerting to see the crucial year 878 commemorated by the single item 'Aed, son of Neill, dies'; though the entry for 877 gives rise to some interesting conjectures. It reads, 'Rhodri, also his son Gwriad, is killed by the Saxons.' What, we may ask, were the Saxons doing killing Rhodri and his son when their time, according to other sources, was fully occupied in fighting the Danes? Did Welsh princes make common cause with the Danes against the ancient enemy?

Our earliest surviving copy of the *Welsh Annals* dates from the late tenth or early eleventh centuries, and the record ends in 977. In the fourteenth century another Welsh work, *Brut y Tywysogion* (*The Chronicle of the Princes of Wales*), was prepared largely by copying from the *Welsh Annals*, though the story is taken to 1066. Little is added to our knowledge of events in the Anglo-Saxon section of Britain by these two books, though they provide a useful check on *The Chronicle* and, incidentally, confirm its accuracy.

Other historical documents are *Historia Regum* ('History of the Kings'), attributed to Simeon of Durham, 1104–1108; *Flores Historiarum* ('Flowers of History'), written by Roger of Wendover in the early thirteenth century; *The Reigns of the Danish Kings of England*, by Florence of Worcester, writing in the early twelfth century; an anonymous *History of St Cuthbert*; and several Frankish monastic chronicles. The ballad of the Battle of Maldon, and several Norse poems, provide interesting background information. Copies of codes of laws prepared by the kings of Kent and by the Wessex monarchs, Ina, Alfred, Athelstan, Edmund, Edgar and Ethelred II, are in existence; as are the treaties made between Alfred and Guthrum and between Ethelred and the Vikings.

Of Anglo-Saxon charters and wills over 80 survive, many of them from the reign of Athelstan. They throw valuable light on local history, as in one by which Athelstan, commemorating a victory over the Danes somewhere near Malmesbury in about 930, gives the town 500 acres of land, by a charter which reads, 'I give and grant to them that royal heath near my little town of Norton, for their aid given to me in my conflict with the Danes.' Most of the places mentioned in these charters and wills can still be identified.

In addition, we have the lives of eight saints, probably more edifying than accurate; more than 50 private letters; several manumission documents; and guild regulations for Cambridge, Exeter, Bedwyn and Abbotsbury. And archaeology, of course, makes its contribution to our understanding of the times.

Some of the literary documents we have are of such high quality that we know at least as much about events in England in these critical centuries as we do of any Continental country. Few other kingdoms have anything comparable to *The Anglo-Saxon Chronicle*.

I

From Hengist to Egbert

Almost certainly the final departure of the Roman legions from Britain in the early years of the fifth century was not regarded by all Britons as an unmitigated disaster. Because we have so few records does not mean that the island relapsed immediately into barbarism. We can appreciate that for some the comparative absence of records, especially of tax records, would have been a welcome relief.

The peace of the British province of the Roman Empire had been brutally shattered by a full-scale converging invasion in 367. Until then the *Beata Tranquillitas* (blessed peace) referred to on London-minted coins of the period had been a reality. In 367 a league of predatory nations, chief of which were the Picts, Scots (from Ireland) and Saxons, assaulted Roman Britain from all sides. Hadrian's Wall was over-run by treachery, and the sea proved a highway for enemy fleets. Throughout 367 and 368 the province was at the mercy of robbers and looters who, after the initial concerted campaign had succeeded, had split into independent gangs, doing whatever evil they willed. In 368 a Roman general Theodosius reappeared at Richborough with fresh troops and, having consolidated his position there, in the following year set about clearing the country of the parasites infesting it. This he accomplished effectively, and Britain tried to resume its former way of life. The casualties, both in human life and in social order, had been enormous but, with Hadrian's Wall restored and new auxiliaries imported from the Rhineland to help guard the province against the still restless Picts and Scots, there seemed a chance of a gradual rebuilding of Roman civilization.

The Roman British had, however, one natural but fatal obsession. They had no conception of their country as a separate state but regarded it as simply an integral part of Rome. As dangers threatened the Empire from other quarters, the troops that might have been defending Britain were called away for more urgent duties. And, in the lulls in the storms of barbarian invasions which were ravaging Europe, the Roman commanders of legions stationed in Britain joined in the scramble for the imperial throne. In 383 one such commander, Maximus, was proclaimed Emperor of Rome by the army in Britain. Four years later he withdrew the garrison from the Wall and went adventuring on the Continent, to claim his crown. He actually succeeded in occupying Rome for a short time but was defeated and killed at Aquileia in 388. Whereupon, in 395, the Irish descended on western Britain and indulged in an orgy of raiding, slave-catching, looting and slaughter.

In 398 a Roman army again appeared on the south coast and set about restoring order, as had happened under Theodosius. The Irish were driven out, and soon afterwards their High King, Niall, was killed. But again the army had to be withdrawn, to face the onslaught of the Goths (who eventually sacked Rome in 410).

In 407 another adventurer, Constantine III, was proclaimed Emperor by such troops as were still in Britain, and again, with no conception of confining himself to Britain, he shipped every soldier he could raise over to Gaul, where he set up court at Arles. There he managed to survive, keeping some sort of imperial state, until 411 when, beset by more powerful commanders, he suddenly felt a call to religion and sought to escape nemesis by becoming a monk. The ruse failed to work, and he was beheaded.

Some students think that they see evidence for yet another re-occupation of Britain by an imperial army in about 418, with a final withdrawal seven years later. Certainly in 446 the Romano-British still living in Britain sent a desperate message to Aëtius, the great Roman general who had recently defeated the Huns, to come and rescue them from the barbarians, but the appeal was in vain. The British had to be left to work out their own salvation.

It is now generally appreciated that the Romans were not a lot of foreigners holding down a province by means of an occupying army. For over 300 years Britain had been an integral part of the one Empire that at that time represented civilization. A Syrian, an Italian, a Greek or an Egyptian felt no sense of being 'abroad' when he came to Britain, nor did a Briton consider himself a foreigner in Rome, Athens or Jerusalem: the empire was cosmopolitan. That having been said, it is also true that the greater part of the population of Britain consisted of the descendants of the ancient Celtic inhabitants. Under the Roman system new provinces were cemented into the Empire by cultivating the local gentry. Generations of British landowning-families received a Roman education and absorbed Roman culture until they thought of themselves as Roman. The third

Constantine may or may not have been a Briton by birth, but he obviously placed his loyalty to the Empire before loyalty to Britain.

Between 407, when Constantine took the bulk of the army of Britain across the Channel into Gaul, and 446, when Roman Britain addressed its last appeal to the rulers of Rome, is a period of nearly 40 years—a human generation. Britain in those years was not stripped of its population. With the soldiers went many of the administrators and civil servants, while fair numbers of citizens, feeling safer on the same side of the sea as Rome, emigrated to Armorica (to which they gave its subsequent name, Britanny). But the bulk of the population remained.

Raids from almost every quarter kept them anxious and tense, but life was not all raids. A man of, shall we say, Oxfordshire, who was born in the early years of the century, may have experienced in his lifetime perhaps a couple of encounters with slave-raiders or pirates, but in the long intervals of peace he would have lived a normal life and raised a family. The raiders were after easy pickings. When they met with resistance, as at the walls of a fortified town or a well-defended villa, they tended to bypass the obstacle. When St. Patrick, having been captured as a boy of sixteen in such a slave raid in Britain, probably in the first decade of the fifth century, eventually escaped from captivity in Ireland and returned after an absence of six years, he found his family still living their normal life in their old home.

What the province, turned adrift from the Empire, lacked was a central authority. Each community, each town or *civitas*, had to work out its own administration and defence. Through the mist of the centuries we can dimly discern a conflict between two groups, or perhaps between two cultures. A section of the aristocracy seems to have staged a Celtic revival and even to have visualised Britain as a Celtic kingdom, under a native king. Opposed to them were the traditional Roman gentry, trained in the stiff Roman school and loyal to all the conventions and organisation of Rome. We even know the names of the two leaders, and where their strength lay. The Celt was Vortigern, or, in the British language, Guorthigirn, whose home apparently was in north Wales but who seems to have had authority over a great part of Britain. He is termed 'King' of Britain, and his dominions certainly extended to Kent. His adversary was Ambrosius Aurelianus, who seems to have controlled some sort of government in the region of the Cotswolds—a little state including the cities of Cirencester, Gloucester and Bath and the galaxy of villas known to have existed there, though there is also archaeological evidence to suggest Somerset as his base. Nennius says that Vortigern was 'beset with fear', not only of the raiding Picts and Scots, but of 'Roman aggression and also by dread of Ambrosius'.

So emerges a pattern of events that become all too familiar in the centuries that were to follow, the divided Britons calling in enemies of other races to aid them in their internecine quarrels. Vortigern, hard-pressed on several fronts, saw no harm in enlisting the services of 'three keels from Germany, driven in exile, in which were Horsa and Hengist, who were brothers'. Vortigern 'received them kindly and handed over to them the island which in their language is called Thanet'. It was a decision for which Vortigern has been denigrated and despised ever since, but it should be remembered that he was not acting without precedent. The Romans had been doing the same thing for centuries, and increasingly so in the preceding century. Great numbers of warriors from the Teutonic tribes beyond the Rhine were enlisted in the Roman armies.

Nor were the Germanic tribes—Saxons, Angles, Jutes or whatever they were called—unknown in Britain. Pirates from across the North Sea were probably raiding the east coast of Britain before ever the first Roman armies crossed the Straits of Dover, and it is likely that during the long Roman era groups of them introduced as mercenaries (known as *foederati*), had settled in the country. The earliest Teutonic objects discovered by archaeologists in Britain have come from Dorchester-on-Thames, from the late fourth century onwards.

Whether Hengist and Horsa were real persons or not, their alleged actions must typify what went on. *The Anglo-Saxon Chronicle* states that they came

first of all to support the Britons, but they afterwards fought against them. The king directed them to fight against the Picts; and they did so; and obtained the victory wheresoever they came. They then sent to the Angles and desired them to send more assistance. They described the worthless-ness of the Britons and the richness of the land. They then sent them greater support. . . .

So the Teutonic peoples from over the North Sea obtained a foothold in Britain.

This was the period of the migration of nations. Driven by pressure from the savage Huns, who had emerged like locusts from the steppes of Asia, the Teutonic tribes of Middle Europe—the Goths, the Suevi, the Alemanni, the Vandals—spilled over the Rhine and Danube, those ancient frontiers of the Empire, and penetrated to its farthest corners. Rotten as a decaying apple, the Empire fell hopelessly to armies less numerous than its own. In most instances the invaders were led by chieftains bearing the Teutonic title of 'King' who, having taken possession of vast territories, proceeded to instal their lieutenants as a new aristocracy. Under the new regime, life in the towns and villages of most of the western part of the Empire went on much as before. Only the rulers had changed.

It seems likely that a similar development was planned for Britain. The stage was set for a take-over on the now well-established pattern. There was on the one hand a weak, disunited but wealthy country, apparently unable to defend itself; on the other, a vigorous group of peoples who were finding their homes on the flat shores from northern Holland to southern Denmark too restricted for their increasing population, who were formidable warriors, who had command of the sea, and who had already established bridgeheads in Britain. Around the middle of the fifth century there was evidently a concerted attempt at the conquest of Britain, with the Angles, Saxons and allied tribes taking the leading part but aided by the Picts, Scots and Irish. One suspects a master-mind, of the calibre of Alaric the Goth and Clovis the Frank, planning and directing the invasion, but his name has not survived.

At first, everything went well for the invaders. Then resistance stiffened, largely it seems through the efforts of Ambrosius, evidently a Roman gentleman and commander of the old school. When he eventually fell, he was succeeded by an even more effective leader whom Gildas, one of our chief authorities, does not mention by name but whom other chroniclers identify as Arthur. The tradition is that Arthur was victorious in 12 great battles, culminating in an overwhelming triumph at 'Mons Badonicus', after which Britain had peace for about 40 years. Much ingenuity has been expended in trying to identify the sites of the battles, the sixth-century British names of which are given but have long ago been superseded and their identity forgotten. The theory that they were widely distributed throughout Britain is probably correct. Modern students have suggested that Arthur may have owed his success to the use of heavy cavalry, brought over from the Continent. The Saxons, who were seafarers rather than horsemen, had no answer to such tactics. After all, it was the heavy-cavalry charge of the Goths that won the battle of Adrianople in the year 378, a lesson that was not lost on the Roman world. We catch an echo of the British cavalry in the legends of 'King' Arthur and his knights.

Whatever else he was, Arthur was not a king; the British records make this plain. In them he is referred to by a number of titles but chiefly as *Dux Bellorum*—Battle Leader. Gildas, in a series of dooms, mentions the names of five kings who were contemporaries of Arthur. They are Constantine of Dumnonia (the south-western peninsula), Aurelius Conanus who apparently inherited the territory of Ambrosius, Vortiporius (or Guortepir) of Demetia (west Wales), Cuneglassus, of north or central Wales, and Maglocunus (or Maelgwyn) of Gwynedd. All are roundly castigated by Gildas for a variety of sins, though their chief shortcoming seems to have been failure to unite in the face of the Saxon enemy. As long as Arthur, who evidently held his command independently of any of them, survived he held the British realm together, but with his death it quickly split again into petty quarrelling kingdoms. It has even been suggested that Arthur, the last British champion of Roman civilization, may have been proclaimed Emperor—a not impossible development.

At any rate, the Saxon invasion was halted. More, the Saxons were apparently driven out of much of the territory they had previously occupied. Among the several clues to the course of events one of the most enigmatic is the Wansdyke, a formidable ditch-and-bank barrier which stretches across the entire width of Wiltshire and extends to the sea in the neighbourhood of Portishead. There is mystery about this mighty trench, more than 50 miles long. Modern archaeologists have pointed out that it is in two sections, and the currently held opinion is that the two were unrelated. They think that the eastern section, in Wiltshire, was probably a division between the Saxons on the Thames and the Saxons of Wiltshire, but that the western section may date from the time of Arthur.

I would have thought that the other way round would have been the more logical explanation, for the Wansdyke faces an enemy to the north, where there were certainly Saxons—on the upper Thames—in Arthurian times. It would seem reasonable to visualise Arthur assembling his troops behind it in preparation for the hammer-blows which chased the invaders back to the eastern sea. After the battle of Mount Badon, which most authorities place near the hill-fort of Liddington on the downland ridge overlooking Swindon, there is some evidence that the victorious Britons pursued the Saxons right across Britain. The Devil's Dyke and Fleam Dyke across the Icknield Way in Cambridgeshire may have been defences thrown up hurriedly by the fugitives; they belong to this period. There are also references to a migration of Angles and Saxons *eastwards* from Britain about this time. Considerable numbers of them apparently left the island and were settled by Theuderic, king of the Franks, in a district of Thuringia. When, many years later, Saxons again found themselves in the vicinity of the Wansdyke they knew nothing of its origin and so attributed it to their god Woden.

It would be a neat way of tying events together, but apparently things were not as simple as that. Present evidence apparently points to a date later than Arthur for the eastern Wansdyke, though what really happened remains obscure.

However, the importance of this preamble is that it demonstrates that the Teutonic plan to effect a quick conquest of Britain in the late fifth and early sixth centuries failed. It was, incidentally, the only country in western Europe where the barbarian invasions did fail. The British commander,

Arthur, was the man who foiled the plan. After he was dead, slain by his own kinsman in one of those internecine squabbles that so demoralised the British, the Saxon advance was resumed. But this time it was not one grand campaign conceived by a military genius. Instead, it was a nibbling away of scraps of territory over a period of several centuries. Mercia, the Saxon kingdom which eventually extended like an amoeba over most of the Midlands, probably took its name from 'merc', a march or boundary. It was a frontier zone—a no-man's-land.

Writing about the middle of the sixth century, at about the time that the Arthurian peace had stabilised the situation in Britain, the Byzantine writer Procopius states:

Three very populous nations possess the island of Britain, and there is a king over each of them. And the names of these nations are the Anglii, and the Friesians, and the Britons who have their name from the island. And so numerous are these nations that every year great numbers, with their wives and children, migrate thence to the Franks, and the Franks give them dwellings in that part of their land which seems most bare of men. . . .

Although Procopius was writing in far-off Constantinople, it seems that he got his information from an embassy which the king of the Franks sent to the emperor there. The picture he gives is of three more-or-less equal peoples living side-by-side in a reasonably prosperous island. Far from having been depopulated by raids and war, the countryside is so over-crowded that the surplus population is forced to emigrate. Here is some corroboration of the contention that after Arthur's victories many of the Anglo-Saxons returned to the Continent, though the statement may also refer to British emigration to Armorica. 'The Friesians', incidentally, is evidently a term used to denote the Saxons; both peoples, if a distinction can be made between them, came from the shores of north-western Germany and north-eastern Holland.

Ambrosius checked the Anglo-Saxon invasion in apparently the last quarter of the fifth century. Arthur fought his campaigns between about 505 and 517, the last being the date usually accepted for the climactic Battle of Mount Badon. The battle of Camlann, in which Arthur fell fatally wounded by his nephew Mordred, occurred in 538. Significantly *The Anglo-Saxon Chronicle*, with a natural reluctance to record the defeats of its own people, has little to say of the period: there are only 12 brief entries for the first 50 years of the sixth century. Most of those entries concern some minor successes attending the West Saxons in Hampshire, who were able to occupy the Isle of Wight.

When the wars are resumed, they are not exclusively between Anglo-Saxons and Britons. The first action occurred in 552 at Sarum, where the

West Saxons defeated the Britons, but three entries (in *The Anglo-Saxon Chronicle*) and 16 years later we find the West Saxons fighting not Britons but fellow-Saxons in Kent. And that was the pattern for the next 250 years—Saxons fought Saxons and Angles as often as they fought Britons; Britons fought Britons as often as they fought Saxons. British kings were courted as allies by Saxons kings in wars against their Saxon neighbours. As early as 633 Penda of Mercia allied himself with Cadwallon, king of Gwynedd, in a merciless campaign against Edwin, the Anglian king of Northumbria. There were civil wars between rival contenders for the crown in both Anglo-Saxon and British states. Britain was thoroughly Balkanised.

The development was of supreme importance in the moulding of England. The swift conquest of former Roman provinces on the Continent by barbarians permitted a continuity of life, traditions and culture that was impossible in fragmented Britain. Each little kingdom, each community, had to hammer out its own traditions, developing in the process a self-reliance and sturdy independence of thought that were to serve the nation well in the future. In the absence of a supreme central authority, common law, which was crystallization of accepted custom, assumed a remarkable importance. A united England was eventually achieved through integration and compromise, processes at which the English have ever since excelled.

Nevertheless, there was from the beginning a somewhat nebulous unifying principle at work. Whether this derived from the knowledge that Britain had once been one country under Roman rule, or whether the concept originated with the Anglo-Saxons themselves is uncertain. Perhaps it came from the nameless leader who planned the first bold campaign that was intended to over-run the whole island, as the Roman provinces of the Continent had been over-run. Whatever the explanation, from the very beginning one of the Anglo-Saxon kings was held to be superior to the others. He was the *Bretwalda*, which means 'ruler of Britain', and there was considerable rivalry for the title. Some authorities have considered that the concept belonged more to the realms of poetry than of practical politics and was a term used by minstrels singing of the deeds of heroes to an audience of courtiers feasting in a hall on a winter's night. However, it was more than that, for there are several instances of a Bretwalda exercising his right to be associated with or over-rule grants made by lesser kings.

The first Bretwalda is Aelle, of the South Saxons. He is succeeded by Ceawlin, of Wessex; then by Ethelbert, of Kent; then by Raedwald of East Anglia; then by three Northumbrian kings, Edwin, Oswald and

Oswy. Egbert of Wessex was the eighth. All of these and the other Anglo-Saxon kings have one common denominator, in that all except one, according to *The Anglo-Saxon Chronicle*, traced their ancestry back to Woden. Woden, although regarded as a god, was also an Anglo-Saxon leader in the German homeland of the tribes and only a few generations removed from the leaders who came to Britain. If nothing else, the position of Bretwalda must have served to remind them of their common ancestry. (The one exception to the rule is provided by the kings of the East Saxons, who ruled in Essex and who traced their ancestry not to Woden but to another god, Seaxnot.)

The kingdoms of Britain in the early seventh century were approximately as follows:

BERNICIA comprised the coastal areas of Northumberland and Durham, westwards to the Pennines, and also the Scottish counties northwards to the Firth of Forth.

DEIRA was, roughly, Yorkshire. Bernicia and Deira were soon afterwards united to form the kingdom of Northumbria.

South of the Humber LINDSEY was occupied by a people known as the Lindisfaran. Their kingdom endured to the very end of the eighth century but gradually became subservient to Mercia.

MERCIA's beginning was in the valley of the lower Trent, from where the Mercians gradually extended their territory into the great forests which covered much of the Midlands.

The MIDDLE ANGLES seem to have occupied territory in what later became the counties of Leicestershire, Northamptonshire, Rutland and Huntingdonshire, but they disappeared early from the scene (by the middle of the seventh century) by incorporation in Mercia.

The EAST ANGLES had their territory in what is still known as East Anglia—the counties of Norfolk and Suffolk. They later came under the overlordship of Mercia and were among the first of the English peoples to feel the depredations of the Danes. In the early centuries East Anglia had considerable power and, as noted, one of its monarchs, Raedwald, was recognised as Bretwalda.

ESSEX remained an independent kingdom for some time, with a dynasty of kings whose names are known. London was in early times its chief town.

The MIDDLE SAXONS, who gave their name to Middlesex, were evidently independent for a time and were later associated with Essex, perhaps as a satellite kingdom. Kent, the section of Britain nearest to the Continent and therefore most susceptible to Continental influences, assumed early importance and long retained it, until finally incorporated in Wessex.

Aelle, king of the SOUTH SAXONS, was the first Bretwalda, but the kingdom which he founded was too hemmed in—by the sea, the marshes to the east and west and the Wealden Forest to the north—to retain great importance. Little is known of its subsequent history, though it apparently had an independent king towards the end of the seventh century.

SURREY, the name being derived from words meaning 'southern land', was for most of its history disputed territory between the kings of Kent, Wessex and Mercia. At times it had an under-king, tributary to one or another of its neighbours.

Concerning the origins of WESSEX, which was eventually to emerge as the dominant kingdom, there is some doubt. Its founding is generally attributed to Cerdic, who landed in 495, but Cerdic is an enigma. His name is Celtic rather than Saxon. *The Anglo-Saxon Chronicle*, admittedly vague about this early period, says that the first West Saxons arrived in three ships in 514. The early kingdom of Wessex seems to have coincided approximately with Hampshire, to which were later added Wiltshire and Berkshire.

North of Wessex a people named the HWICCES occupied what is now Gloucestershire and Worcestershire; their name survives in Wychwood Forest. Inevitably, they were absorbed in Mercia.

At some time in the seventh century the plains of Herefordshire and southern Shropshire were occupied by a people named the MAGONSAETAN, of whom little is known. For a time they had their own royal family, but their kings seem to have been subject to the Mercians.

Of the British (Celtic) states, DUMNONIA occupied the greater part of the south-western peninsula, including almost all Somerset until 658. Dorset apparently remained under British control until about that date, though whether as an independent state or as a satellite of Dumnonia is not known.

Wales was divided into a number of states, chief of which were GWENT, DYFOR, POWYS and GWYNEDD.

In midland England two British kingdoms held out for a long time.

In the Chilterns a British enclave was still in existence until the year 571, when *The Anglo-Saxon Chronicle* recorded, 'This year Cuthulf fought with the Britons at Bedford and took four towns, Lenbury, Aylesbury, Benson and Eynsham.' Parts of the enclave may have survived even later.

Farther north, the British kingdom of ELMET, in southern Yorkshire, served as a barrier between Northumbria (Deira) and Mercia until Edwin conquered it, in the late 620s.

At some time during the second half of the seventh century the kings of Northumbria apparently reached the western sea, splitting off Cumbria, the ancient REGED, from Strathclyde. At the same time Irish settlers had a state of their own, DALRIADA, in Argyllshire. North of these regions lay the kingdom of the PICTS, which does indeed seem to have been one kingdom and not a conglomeration of tribes. But the situation in the north is confused, for around the year 650 the Picts had an Anglian king, Talorcan, the grandson of a king of Bernicia. Such were the ingredients of the British stew in the seventh century: the cauldron was always simmering.

In the first half of the seventh century the most active Anglo-Saxon states were those of the south, notably Wessex, but later the spotlight shifts to Northumbria. At the beginning of the century the kingdom of Bernicia was so weak that it could do no more than hold on to the coastal strip around Bamborough, for it is recorded by Nennius that Celtic kings penetrated as far as Holy Isle, where they were besieged for three days and nights. Under a king named Ethelfrith, however, the power of Bernicia rapidly increased, to the extent that his armies crossed the Pennines and occupied much of Lancashire and Cumbria, defeating the north Welsh in a bloody battle at Chester.

In 616 an army led by Raedwald, the Bretwalda, defeated and killed Ethelfrith near the southern frontier of Deira, at the spot where the Roman road from Lincoln crosses the river Idle. Raedwald was on his way to restore Edwin, a royal refugee who had been living at his court, to the throne of Deira, and the battle was so conclusive that the Bernicians too accepted Edwin as their king.

Edwin was a great warrior. He invaded North Wales, occupied both the Isle of Man and Anglesey and shut up Cadwallon, king of Gwynedd, in the islet of Priestholm. But Cadwallon had sufficient strength to strike back. He formed an alliance with Penda, king of Mercia, and the combined British and Anglo-Saxon armies descended on Northumbria. Edwin was defeated and slain at the battle of Hatfield Chase, and Cadwallon wreaked a cruel and bloodthirsty revenge for all the wrongs of his race on helpless Northumbria. The carnage and destruction continued for more than a year, until Oswald, a relation of Edwin, met and killed Cadwallon.

Oswald then became ruler of a united Northumbria and a very effective monarch, for he was recognised as Bretwalda and, within a few years of his death, was regarded as a saint. After a reign of eight years, old enmities were renewed with Mercia, and the Mercian king, Penda, defeated and killed him at the battle of Maserfelth (which may be Oswestry). Penda thus became by far the strongest monarch in Britain, though not officially recognised as Bretwalda. Hostilities flared again in 654 when Penda, having been annoyed by border harassment by Oswy, the new king of Northumbria, set out with an army of (according to Bede) 'thirty legions', to put a stop to his nonsense. The old alliance with the Britons still held, for on this expedition Penda was accompanied by Cadafael, king of Gwynedd.

But Penda miscalculated and was completely routed by Oswy, with inferior forces, at the battle of Winwaed somewhere near Leeds. Both Penda and an East Anglian king who had supported him were killed, and Cadafael barely escaped with his life.

Oswy now had things all his own way for about three years. He annexed Mercia and the territory of the Middle Angles and was recognised as overlord of all the English kingdoms. But after three years a son of Penda, named Wulfhere, appeared in Mercia and claimed his father's kingdom. His revolt was successful, and Oswy retired to Northumbria and occupied the rest of his life, till his death in 670, with good works. His quiescence allowed Wulfhere to build up his position in southern England until, when Oswy died, he had obtained the allegiance of most of the southern states. Predictably, he could not resist trying conclusions with Oswy's successor, Ecgfrith, but it did him little good. After winning one battle each, the two kings retired each to his own territory, and peace reigned along the border. Ecgfrith thereupon embarked on adventures elsewhere. He invaded the Pictish kingdom of Scotland, annexing much of it, and was recognised as overlord by the British of Strathclyde and the Irish of Dalriada. In 684 he even had the temerity to attempt a sea invasion of Ireland—perhaps more properly described as a piratical raid, for it did little more than devastate much of the kingdom of Meath and earn the hostility of the Irish. Still euphoric with the success of that expedition, Ecgfrith ventured again into Scotland but this time was completely defeated, with the loss of his own life, in a battle at Nechtanesmere near Forfar. The date was 685, and it marks the end of the predominance of Northumbria among the English kingdoms.

Thereafter, under a series of undistinguished kings, Northumbria kept strictly within its own southern borders, though to the north and west it indulged in occasional forays into British, Celtic and Pictish lands. We read, for instance, of an expedition into Strathclyde in 756, when the Northumbrians had the Picts as their allies. The Northumbrian annals contain, too, frequent accounts of palace revolutions and civil wars.

In the meantime the power of Wessex, in the south, had been growing. The early history of Wessex is obscure, and contains a curious incident at its very beginning. *The Anglo-Saxon Chronicle* records for the year 495:

This year came two leaders into Britain, Cerdic, and Cynric his son, with five ships, at a place that is called *Cerdic's*-ore. And they fought with the Welsh the same day.

Now, Cerdic is a British not an Anglo-Saxon name; it corresponds to Caradoc. Cerdic was not a West Saxon and, as noted above, the *Chronicle* also states that the West Saxons first came to Britain, in three ships, in 514. Then, in 519, we read,

This year Cerdic and Cynric undertook the government of the West Saxons; the same year they fought with the Britons at a place now called Charford. From that day have reigned the children of the West Saxon kings.

And that is true, down to the present day, for English monarchs trace their ancestry back to Cerdic. But who Cerdic was remains a mystery, perhaps an opportunist of mixed British and Saxon parentage. An imaginative reconstruction of his life and career is given in Alfred Duggan's novel, *The Conscience of the King*.

After initial campaigns against the British, including one in 571 against the British enclave in the Chilterns and another, in 577, which resulted in the capture of Gloucester, Bath and Cirencester, the kings of the West Saxons became more preoccupied with their Anglo-Saxon neighbours. We read of a campaign against the South Saxons, of another against Penda of Mercia, and of the involvement of the king of the West Saxons in a plot to assassinate King Edwin of Northumbria. In 645 we learn that King Kenwalch of Wessex was 'driven from his dominion by King Penda'. He seems to have returned three years later but apparently had learned his lesson, for instead of indulging in reprisals against the Mercians he turned his attention to his British neighbours in Dyvnaint (Dumnonia). In a campaign in 658 he broke through the barrier of the Forest of Selwood and occupied a large part of Somerset.

More trouble with Mercia followed soon afterwards, and, having won a battle against Kenwalch, King Wulfhere of Mercia marched right through Wessex, invaded the Isle of Wight and gave it to the king of the South Saxons. The frontier between Mercia and Wessex seems to have been firmly established along the Thames and thus, with such a strong power to the north, the kings of Wessex had to look westwards for scope for expansion. In 682 a Wessex king, Kentwine, pushed his kingdom's frontier still farther into Dyvnaint 'pursuing the Britons to the sea'.

Five years later a headstrong youngster who claimed the throne of Wessex collected a small army of similar young men and set about avenging the insult represented by Wulfhere's gift of the Isle of Wight to the king of Sussex. They invaded Sussex and killed the king of that country; they harried the Isle of Wight; then they moved on to Kent where they also 'spread devastation'. The name of the leader of this expedition was Caedwalla, another British name occurring in the royal Wessex dynasty and giving renewed fodder for speculation. After a disaster in which his brother Mull was ambushed in a hut in Kent and burnt to death, Caedwalla went on a pilgrimage to Rome, where he died soon after receiving baptism. His successor was King Ina, a man of considerable ability and reputation. He reigned for 37 years and promulgated an impressive code of laws. He also completed the conquest of Devonshire, but whether or for how long he held complete supremacy over all the kingdoms south of the Thames is not known. In 726 King Ina abdicated and went on a pilgrimage to Rome where, like Caedwalla, he died. The following kings of Wessex were undistinguished persons who enjoyed short reigns, and Mercia again took the lead. For a time in the middle of the eighth century a Mercian king, Ethelbald, was apparently recognised as overlord of all the kingdoms south of the Humber. After reigning for 41 years (a reign of remarkable length for those stormy days) he was assassinated in 757 and was succeeded, after a short civil war, by a scion of the royal house, Offa.

This Offa was one of the great kings of Saxon England. He reigned until 796, acquiring kingdom after kingdom by conquest or treaty until he was justifiably able to term himself, in legal documents, 'King of the English'. He corresponded on equal terms with Continental monarchs, including the great Charlemagne, and constructed along the Welsh border that prodigious earthwork which still survives and bears his name, Offa's Dyke. His correspondence with Charlemagne demonstrates that at that distant time there was already considerable trade between the English kingdoms and the Continent and that in it the export of cloth occupied an important role.

Offa was a considerable marriage-broker. One of his daughters was married to the king of Northumbria, another to Beorhtric, king of Wessex; a third was due to marry the son of Charlemagne, but those negotiations fell through. None of his many relations was disposed to challenge the authority of the patriarchal figure at the head of the family, and Offa completed his reign in peace.

At the court of Charlemagne in those final years of the eighth century was a young prince named Egbert, an exile of the royal house of Wessex. He was apparently in Charlemagne's favour and accompanied the great Emperor in his German wars. The reason for his being a refugee at the imperial court was that he had contested with Beorhtric for the throne of Wessex but had fled when Offa supported his rival. With Offa dead he watched for an opportunity to return. His chance came in 802, when Beorhtric died. Reappearing in Wessex, he was immediately proclaimed king and Cenwulf, the new king of Mercia, evidently thought it diplomatic not to interfere. Cenwulf, however, kept control of the rest of southern England including Kent, East Anglia, Sussex and Essex as well as Mercia, and he felt strong enough to engage in several campaigns against the Welsh. He and his successor Ceolwulf penetrated even into the fastnesses of Snowdon, and the *Welsh Annals* lament, for the year 822, 'Deganwy is destroyed by the Saxons, and they took the region of Powys into their own power.'

Egbert of Wessex bided his time and built up his strength. King Ceolwulf was deposed, and a new king Beornwulf reigned instead over Mercia. In the year 825 (or 823 according to *The Chronicle*) Egbert was ready. He overthrew Beornwulf in a tremendous battle at a place called Ellendun and prepared to assume the overlordship of all England. We have arrived at the time of the entrance on the stage of the first of our Warrior Kings of Saxon England.

From this brief summary of events in these formative centuries we have omitted one important thread, namely, the conversion of the Anglo-Saxons to Christianity. The sequence of political events having now been established, we can see better how the ecclesiastical ones fitted in.

As is well known, Augustine was sent on his mission to the court of Kent in the year 596 but, as is also widely appreciated, that was not the beginning of Christianity in Britain. There were certainly Christians in Britain in the second century A.D. and probably in the first. Indeed, a phrase in the writings of Gildas has been translated (though it is not without ambiguity) to read that 'these islands received the beams of light, that is, the holy precepts of Christ, the true Sun, in the latter part, as we know, of the reign of Tiberius Caesar'. As Tiberius Caesar died in A.D. 37, that would put the coming of Christianity to Britain within a very few years of the death and resurrection of Christ. At the beginning of the third century Tertullian, the Roman author, claimed that Christianity had spread to parts of Britain inaccessible to Roman arms—in other words, to the highlands of Scotland. And Gildas states that, after the end of the persecution by Diocletian in 303, large numbers of Christian churches were rebuilt. We know the names of three martyrs who perished in that persecution; they are Alban of Verulamium, and Aaron and Julius of Caerleon.

Legend and romance have been busy with the esoteric islet of Glastonbury in those early days. The foundation of the little church there, which was succeeded by the mighty Abbey of Glastonbury, has been credited to (a) Aristobulus, one of the 70 disciples commissioned by Christ; (b) St. Philip; (c) two missionaries, Fagan and Deruvian who, however, lived in the late second century; (d) St. Peter; (e) St. Simon Zelotes; (f) Joseph of Arimathea; and (g) Christ himelf. Of them all, the traditions associated with Joseph of Arimathea, though late in appearing in documentary form, are the most tenacious, and there are numerous circumstantial details about his mission. As for the tradition that Christ came to Glastonbury in the hidden years before He began His ministry, we find it embedded in Blake's well-known hymn 'And did those feet, in ancient times'.

For the purpose of our history it is sufficient to emphasise that the arrival of the Christian message in Britain occurred at a very early date. By the time the Anglo-Saxon invasion was gathering momentum, the British Church had already behind it a history of several centuries. It had many churches and a staff of bishops, representatives of whom attended Church councils on the Continent. It had even thrown up its own heretic, a churchman named Pelagius, who preached a doctrine of tolerance and commonsense that modern men would find attractive but which earned him and his followers excommunication by the Pope. In his own day he was so popular that the Pope sent an envoy, Germanus, over to Britain to try to confute the heretics. They met at Verulamium in the year 429, and Germanus not only apparently got the better of the argument but afterwards further strengthened his position by leading the British forces in a successful battle against the Saxons.

However, as the years passed, links with the Roman Church became more and more tenuous. Travel was difficult and perilous and the British, driven back to the western hills and mountains, tended to look wootwards rather than to the south. Britain was being weaned at last from Rome, in ecclesiastical as well as in secular matters. A notable factor in this development was the conversion of the Irish in which, as we know, St. Patrick played a leading part. Born at some time between 370 and 390 A.D. at a locality on the west coast of Britain (considered by various authorities to be by the Firth of Clyde, Solway Firth, in south Wales or on the Somerset side of the Bristol Channel), Patrick was captured by Irish raiders when aged about sixteen and spent six years as a slave in Ireland, working as a shepherd for a man named Miliuc. During his period of captivity he became familar with Irish ways and the Irish language and also received a call to the religious life. After making his escape he underwent a long period of training in Gaul and Italy and became a priest. In 432 he was sent by the Pope to attempt the conversion of Ireland.

That his mission was successful is well known. Ireland became Christian. Almost immediately, the Irish genius, which had already expressed itself in exquisite art, grew into a renaissance. Painting, music and literature flourished, and intrepid Irish voyagers set out to explore beyond the confines of the known world. They were not now raiders bent on acquiring treasure and slaves, but missionaries carrying the Christian gospel. It is known that they reached the Faeroes, Iceland and Greenland, and suspicions are growing that they may have formed settlements on the mainland of America as well. They sent missions, too, to western Scotland and to the barbarian nations of Europe. One of the modern cantons of Switzerland, St. Gall, is named after an Irish missionary of this period. Best known of all the Irish missionaries is St. Columba, who founded a monastery on Iona. Born in 521, he was a younger contemporary of Arthur, the British leader, and he died the year after St. Augustine landed in Kent.

Here, then, was a fresh civilization springing up in a country that had never been dominated by Rome. True, the Irish Church had been founded by an emissary of the Roman Church and owed allegiance to it, but from the beginning it developed in its own Celtic way. Irish society was tribal, with few if any permanently inhabited towns. The Roman system of bishops, each with his diocese centred on a city, therefore fitted awkwardly in Ireland. Monasticism proved more congenial to the Irish. Christian monasticism had begun in Egypt, one of the most celebrated of the early monks being St. Anthony, who retired to an abandoned desert fort and there lived in solitude for many years. This was in the first half of the fourth century. During his lifetime many other men followed his example and became hermits. Later the movement spread like a stubble-fire over all the Roman world, from the Caucasus to the Atlantic. The solitary hermit joined himself with others to form religious communities whose members lived hard, comfortless lives, tending the soil, doing all kinds of manual work and subject to rigid discipline. And, as the civilized world collapsed around them with the barbarian invasions, the monasteries survived as islands of hope in the chaos. Within the monastery-walls monks painstakingly copied ancient manuscripts and saved much of the heritage of the past for posterity, while other devoted brothers kept alive such varied arts as medicine, husbandry and painting. Without their self-sacrificial lives, our modern world would be immeasurably poorer.

From early days Irish Christianity seems to have had direct links with eastern churches rather than through the medium of Rome. It adopted, for example, the eastern method of calculating the date of Easter. In a later century, the seventh, when the new creed of Islam surged through the Middle East and along the shores of North Africa, threatening to eradicate the Christian faith, many refugees fled to the far west, bringing to Ireland their precious skills and equally precious manuscripts. At a time when much of Europe was still barbarous, Ireland had an impressive body of scholars in Latin, Greek and the sciences of the ancient world.

In one other respect the Irish missions differed from most of those of contemporary Rome. Faced all over the Continent with the collapse of the old order and the appearance of new rulers, the Roman church quite naturally tended to concentrate its efforts at the point where they seemed to be most effective. It quickly appreciated that when the rulers of the new kingdoms accepted Christianity their subjects were expected to do the same . . . or else. Like Olaf of Norway who in a later age (the eleventh century) certainly gave his subjects a free choice—they could choose between becoming Christians or dying. The missions of the Roman Church therefore tended to be to kings and courts, as with St. Augustine's mission to the court of Kent. The results seemed to vindicate the approach, in that within a very short time entire populations became at least nominally Christian.

The appeal of the Irish missionaries was, on the other hand, largely to the common people. They did not neglect the kings and princes but gave equal attention to the artisans and peasants. They were simple, humble, devoted souls, converting by the transparent goodness of their lives as well as by preaching. They tramped barefoot over the hills of the north and west, and when the king of Northumbria, Oswald, gave Aidan, one of the best-loved missionaries, a horse to carry him, Aidan promptly gave the horse to the first beggar he met.

So, as the take-over of Britain by the Anglo-Saxons proceeded, three separate Christian churches were at work in the island.

The BRITISH CHURCH, confined to the western third of Britain, had become introspective and isolated. Cut off by barbarian inroads—on the Continent as well as in Britain—from regular contact with Rome, it had turned to Ireland, by which it was strongly influenced. Like the Irish Church, it veered towards monasticism. An early Welsh triad, dating from between 500 and 554 A.D., lists

The three Perpetual Choirs of Britain: the choir of Llan Iltud Vawr in Glamorganshire, the choir of Ambrosius in Ambresbury, and the choir of Glastonbury. In each of these choirs there were 2400 saints, that is there were a hundred for every hour of the day and night in rotation.

The numbers may not be accurate, but one gets the idea. At these centres praise was offered unceasingly by choirs operating on a shift system. It is interesting that an ancient tradition identifies St. Patrick as the first abbot of Glastonbury.

Not surprisingly, in view of the savagery of the pagan Anglo-Saxons, the British Christians in the early centuries of the conquest regarded them with implacable hostility. When, later, the Anglo-Saxons accepted Christianity they held it against the British that the latter had never attempted to introduce them to the Gospel, but there was certainly some excuse for the failure. However, when the West Saxons came to Glastonbury in 658 they were already Christians and the transition seems to have been effected painlessly. The Saxon king, Kenwalch, left the British abbot in possession, and his successors made large grants of land to the Abbey.

The IRISH CHURCH, in contrast to the British, was enthusiastically missionary. The legends of the Cornish saints abound in stories of holy men who came over from Ireland or South Wales, floating on their altars. The statement appears ridiculous if we visualise stone altars but not if we realise that the missionaries travelled in coracles or similar skin boats which, on arrival on a strange shore, could be turned over and used as altars.

A natural field for Irish missionary endeavour was the kingdom of Dalriada, corresponding approximately to the county of Argyllshire, which had been founded by Scots emigrating from Ulster. It was evangelised by St. Columba and his disciples operating from their base on Iona. To Iona in 634 the Northumbrian king, Oswald, sent for a bishop to help restore the shattered realm after the devastation of the campaign by the Welsh king Cadwallon. The missionary bishop who arrived in response to the appeal was Aidan, a saintly man who worked in Northumbria for the next 20 years, establishing as his base an island not unlike Iona—the island of Lindisfarne—where he lived a life of typically monastic asceticism.

From Lindisfarne other evangelists moved into the still pagan kingdoms to the south. Mercia was won for Christianity by Irish bishops from Northumbria, and an Irish-trained priest, Cedd, or Chad, evangelised the East Saxons in Essex. Cedd was a product of Lindisfarne, but another Celt, Fursa, who established a hermit's cell in East Anglia and exercised a considerable influence on the Church in that kingdom, came directly from Ireland.

The principal impact of the ROMAN CHURCH was in Kent, where Augustine and about 40 companions arrived in 597, sent by Pope Gregory the Great. About nine years earlier the Kentish king, Ethelbert, had married a Frankish princess who, being Christian, had brought her own priests with her. Augustine apparently came at a royal invitation, and the conversion was primarily a palace affair—at least, at first. Some of King Ethelbert's subjects accepted Christianity, doubtless from mixed motives; some remained pagan.

Augustine does not appear as a likeable character. He was not fired by missionary zeal. He had not wanted to come to Britain and, once there, had been nervous about how to proceed. Aware that there were already many

Christians in the western part of the island, he arranged a meeting with their leaders. With many reservations on both sides the two parties met at Aust, by the river Severn. The British delegation, incensed by Augustine's arrogant manner, decided to put him to a test. If, when they next entered the conference chamber, he rose to greet them, they would accept that he had true Christian humility and would continue the discussions. If he did not, they would regard him as unfriendly and walk out. Augustine remained in his chair, and the conference broke up. That, at any rate, was the story narrated by Bede, who, being an Anglo-Saxon, could not have been accused of bias towards the Britons, but one suspects that it is not the entire tale. In a complicated situation such as this there were doubtless faults on both sides.

In the generation after Augustine a Kentish princess married King Edwin of Northumbria and, as had happened in Kent, the Christian bride introduced her religion into her new realm. From Canterbury a priest, freshly consecrated bishop, was sent north and within a few years many of the Northumbrians had accepted Christianity. Paulinus also evangelised Lindsey, then a separate kingdom. Meantime other missionaries from Rome arrived to work in East Anglia (where the evangelist was a Burgundian named Felix) and Wessex, whose first bishop was Birinus, who founded a bishopric at Dorchester-on-Thames.

The church in Northumbria received an appalling setback with the invasion of that kingdom by the pagan king Penda of Mercia and the Welsh Cadwallon in 632/33. The Welsh chieftain disgraced his profession of Christianity by his merciless slaughter of the Northumbrians after defeating them in battle. An heroic deacon named James remained at York throughout that terrible year, but very few of his flock survived with him. Under the new king, Oswald, after the death in battle of Cadwallon, the work of conversion had to start all over again and, as related above, the churchman whom Oswald brought in to undertake the task was not a Roman from the south but Aidan, of the Irish Church.

Under Aidan and his successors the church in Northumbria became firmly established. One of the early ecclesiastical foundations was that of Whitby, then known as Streoneshalh, the first and most celebrated abbess of which was Hilda, of the royal Northumbrian family. There in 663 a noteworthy conference was held between the protagonists of the Roman and Celtic customs in the church and the beginnings of a compromise worked out, though at the time the victory seemed to be conclusively with the Romanists led by a dogmatic bishop, Wilfred.

By about 670 every English kingdom, with the exception of Sussex, was nominally Christian, as were the British kingdoms to the west. Among the ordinary populace, however, pagan customs and beliefs continued to flourish. Nevertheless, the spread of Christianity was not entirely a matter of baptising kings and nobles. That was a first step, but it was followed by evangelical missions to the common people. There survives an attractive reminiscence of St. Aldhelm, first bishop of Sherborne (who died aged 74 or 75 in the year 709 A.D.) on missionary journeys in the Forest of Selwood, a wild region in Wessex. A tall, sturdy, red-faced old man (he was seventy when he became bishop), he would stride through the forest accompanied by five or six monks. He carried an ash-stick as a staff, and over his shoulder a harp was slung. When he came to some strategic spot, such as a village green or a bridge, he would sit down, gather his disciples around him, and proceed to sing and play popular songs or songs of his own composition. When he had a congregation he would launch into a sermon, with hell-fire as a prominent theme. He would conclude the proceedings by baptising the alarmed and somewhat bewildered peasants in a convenient stream. Aldhelm was an enthusiastic musician. In his abbey at Malmesbury he installed what was said to be the first organ in England, 'a mighty instrument with innumerable tones, blown with bellows and enclosed in a gilded case'.

The old wild days of paganism were passing. At Whitby the first great English poet, the herdsman Caedmon who was too shy to sing until commanded to do so in a vision, was composing verses about the Creation. At Canterbury an outstanding archbishop, Theodore, was establishing a school in which Latin, music, arithmetic and astronomy were taught. Monks in the monasteries and abbeys were engaged in producing exquisite illuminated manuscripts; masons were erecting and decorating lovely stone churches and village crosses. Cuthbert, one of the earliest nature conservationists, was so gentle and trusted that the eider- ducks of Lindisfarne would come waddling up to him to be fondled. In his cell at Jarrow Bede, who achieved a reputation as one of the greatest scholars of Christendom, translated the Gospels into English and produced, among his prolific writings, his invaluable *Ecclesiastical History of the English People*. It was the first exuberant blossoming of the English genius.

As with the Irish after their conversion, so the new English Christians felt impelled to spread the gospel to heathen peoples beyond the sea. Within less than 100 years after Augustine's landing in Kent English missionaries, notably Wilfred and Willibrord, were active in Frisia, to be followed in 716 by the greatest of the English missionaries to heathen central Europe, Boniface. By birth Boniface was a West Saxon named Wynfrith, from what is now Devonshire, and many West Saxons went over to join him in his evangelising work in the German forests.

The eighth century in Britain was thus, on the whole, a period of peace, prosperity and progress. Squabbles and petty wars between the kingdoms persisted, but between them were intervals of tranquillity. Large settlements, the embryos of future towns, were springing up, arts and trade were flourishing, and the monasteries were oases of creative culture. Men, looking back at it, regarded it as a golden age and envied their fortunate forefathers who had lived in it and had had no foreboding of the tempest that was to come.

II

The Anglo-Saxons

One of the details which every schoolboy learns about the Battle of Hastings is that when King Harold fell his 'housecarles' fought on till every man of them was killed. Although the 'housecarles', under that name, came into prominence under the Danish kings of England, similar bodyguards of warriors had long been associated with the kings of the English kingdoms. Their outstanding characteristic was an intense personal loyalty to their leader. To survive the death of their king in battle was held to be disgraceful.

In early Anglo-Saxon documents the bodyguard is known by an Anglo-Saxon word (*gesith*) which means 'companion'. It describes exactly their role in early English society: they accompanied the king on his journeyings. For their services they were rewarded in various ways but notably by grants of land, and they thus became a landed aristocracy. When they were not actually with the king they were representing him in other parts of his kingdom.

It should be remembered that the period from the landing of Hengist on Thanet to the death of Harold at Hastings is more than 550 years—a period which, if measured from our own time, would take us back to the Battle of Agincourt. Innumerable changes and developments naturally occurred during those long years. The instinctive loyalty to a leader is, however, an abiding feature. It may have had its origin in the discipline of a ship's crew. The three maritime nations which, according to Bede, invaded Britain from over the North Sea were the Angles, the Saxons and the Jutes. That they regarded themselves as distinct peoples is illustrated, as several authorities have pointed out, by the fact that of two kingdoms which were established side-by-side in the eastern part of Britain one called themselves the East Saxons (Essex) and the other the East Angles (East Anglia). Their cultures were very similar, however, and there is uncertainty about their respective countries of origin. All that can be said is that all of them came from the flat, marshy shores of north-western Europe between the mouth of the Rhine and the Danish peninsula.

Procopius (*see* p. 12) mentions yet another nation which he thought occupied part of Britain in the sixth century, the Friesians. They are evidently synonymous with the Saxons for him though, in fact, it is possible to distinguish between them. According to present evidence, the Friesians were the nation occupying the coastal strip of marshland between the mouth of the Elbe and the mouth of the Rhine around the opening of the Christian era. In a parallel zone on the higher land behind them lived the Old Saxons. At that time the coast was slowly sinking. Winter storms breached the mudbank and sandbars and sent the grey waters of the North Sea pouring inland to form new bays and lagoons. The Friesians defended their homes with embankments of timber and earth, progressively raised over the centuries to form artificial islands, known as *terpen*. At the same time as they were thus under pressure from the sea they were also losing, or having to share, territory with their landward neighbours. In this age of the Migration of Nations populous tribes were moving across Germany, themselves under pressure from other nations farther east—the most formidable of which were, of course, the Huns sweeping westwards from their home on the steppes of Central Asia. The general effect of this traffic was to elbow the Saxons towards the coast, where they mingled with the Friesians. And the natural consequence was overcrowding in the coastal settlements.

Piracy was a tradition in the North Sea—as, indeed, elsewhere in the ancient world. From the end of the second century A.D. at least Saxon pirates and raiders were active. As long as the Empire was strong and the coastal defences firmly manned and managed they were little more than an occasional nuisance, but as Rome weakened so the raiders grew stronger. The early Anglo-Saxon raiders were doubtless adventurous young men for whom there were small prospects in their overcrowded homeland. Living on man-made islands in a waste of water and marshland, they were doubtless more or less amphibious from childhood. Their sea-going boats, clinker-built and without decks, were up to 70 or 80 ft. long, with 14 or 16 oars on either side, plus a steering paddle. A ship's crew would thus number between 30 or 40.

The young Anglo-Saxons who manned these ships were wild, reckless, bloodthirsty ruffians. Unlike many of the central European peoples who poured into the Roman Empire in its age of decline, they had been untouched by Roman civilisation. They had no use for cities, stone buildings or any civilised art. War was to them an end in itself; they exulted in battle, both with human enemies and with the stormy forces of nature. As the Britons learned to their cost, they delighted in launching an attack at the height of a storm, when prudent men stayed indoors. In honour of their savage gods they sacrificed every tenth captive in the roaring waves of the sea-shore. Afterwards, drunk with mead in their timber halls, they boasted of their deeds in songs which reeked with allusions to gory blades, ravens dipping their beaks in blood, 'arrows sleeting like hail', and the joys, in another world, of heroes who fell in battle.

A boat full of such men would depend for success on unwavering co-operation between them. In practical terms, it would call for complete trust in and obedience, in times of stress, to a leader. The same loyalty was, in later times, transferred to war-leaders who commanded a fleet of boats or any army of men and so, by a natural transition, to kings.

As the Empire foundered, so these joyous, brutal raiders conceived the idea of permanent settlement in lands which offered better opportunities than those of their congested mudbanks. It seems that they first set their target in northern Gaul, which meant simply hedge-hopping westwards along the coast. Unfortunately for that programme another nation got there first. The Franks, a Teutonic nation cascading across the Rhine, were able to take over the old Roman province virtually intact and, once in possession, were energetic in keeping other claimants out.

So the Anglo-Saxons turned to Britain. There is now archaeological evidence for the existence of Saxon mercenaries in Britain by the late fourth century. Such historical records as we have point to Kent as the earliest settlement by the invaders. It seems evident that from the end of the fifth century, when Hengist was establishing a base in Thanet, a wholesale migration to the east coast occurred. Here the newcomers found a countryside not unlike their homeland—a relatively flat land traversed by slow-flowing rivers which made admirable highways. In particular they advanced up the Thames, the Humber, the rivers which flow into The Wash and the smaller rivers of East Anglia. On pages 10–12 are reminders that the advance was not without its vicissitudes. Indeed, many of the first settlers were apparently so discouraged by the spirited resistance of the Britons that they returned to Germany. Those who hung on for a generation, however, were rewarded by new opportunities provided by the internal squabbles of the Britons, and the settlements along the eastern shores of Britain soon cohered into a group of kingdoms.

In their settlements the same discipline and spirit of co-operation which served them so well on board ship continued in evidence. The Anglo-Saxons were good farmers—probably better than the Britons, even when the latter were under the influence of Rome. The early Anglo-Saxon settlement normally divided the land around it, reclaimed from forest marsh or whatever its primitive state, into two great fields (later, three of more), one of which was devoted to crops, the other to fallow. In the following year the fallow field was cropped and the cropped one rested. Each field was divided into long, narrow strips of an acre or so, each allocated to individual families according to status and other considerations. The strips were seldom contiguous to each other but were well distributed over the great field, so that no one peasant should monopolise the best land. Ploughing and other major operations were a communal effort, but each family harvested the crops on its own strips. The crops grown were wheat, barley, oats and flax, with perhaps a few vegetables in garden plots.

In addition, the Anglo-Saxons kept the usual domestic animals including cattle, sheep, pigs and geese. These were pastured on the common land beyond the arable fields, the pigs in particular foraging in the woods. Although they were owned by individual peasants, they were probably managed on a communal basis, with a village cow-herd, swine-herd, goose-herd and so on.

The dwellings of the early Anglo-Saxon peasants were miserable huts, tent-shaped and without walls at the sides. The floor was of beaten earth, several inches below the level of the surrounding soil. The roofs were of thatch and the gable-ends of wattle, perhaps plastered with mud. These huts were generally arranged in no sort of pattern, according to the evidence of those so far examined archaeologically, though erected fairly close together for protection and companionship. Each probably had its private yard or close, surrounded by a hedge.

In some, though not in all villages, a person of higher rank had a hall. This resembled in most respects a typical English barn of later date. It was long in relation to its breadth, and had low walls and a high-pitched roof with either gabled or rounded ends. The roof was of thatch, the walls either of boards or of wattle-and-plaster, the frame of massive forest timbers. Some halls may have had a watch-tower. Internal divisions were few, though occasionally separate sleeping-quarters were provided for the owner or for the women.

In the early English kingdoms were four principal classes of men. The free peasants, or *ceorls*, whose hovels have just been described, comprised the bulk of the population. The nobles, who lived in the halls, could be either king's companions who had been rewarded with a grant of land or had been sent to some strategic locality for reasons of defence, or they could be formerly independent leaders who had found it expedient to throw in their lot with a more powerful king.

At the top of the social scale sat the king; at the bottom were the slaves.

How numerous the latter were is not known. Some of them were undoubtedly Britons captured in raids and wars, but not all the Britons became slaves when their country was taken over. In numerous places all over England are found place-names incorporating the element 'Welsh', and usually they refer to a hamlet or satellite of a larger English settlement. Here the Britons (or 'Welsh' to the Saxons) continued to exist as poor relations of the victorious invaders. The laws of certain Saxon kings, notably Ina of Wessex, recognise the existence and rights, though on a lower level than their English neighbours, of these British survivors. Calculated by *wergild*, the amount payable in compensation to the families of men slain, the Welsh had about half the value of the English.

The concepts of aristocracy among the northern peoples rested on the principle of protection. In a violent age when might tended to be right, ordinary citizens who earned their living by the arts and skills of peace were willing to pay part of their income for protection. That, at least, was the theory, though usually they had little choice.

The noble, or thane, in the hall was entitled to have his neighbours do his share of the work in the common fields, on the assumption that he had to be ready at all times to take up arms in their defence. The principle was extended further to cater for the needs of a king and his court. In the early centuries, when towns were few and villages the norm, the king was peripatetic, moving from place to place largely in order not to exhaust the provisions of any locality and also to keep in touch with his people. Royal domains were distributed throughout the realm. When the king and his retinue arrived at any one of them they could call on the other villages in the neighbourhood to deliver their tribute in kind. An early rough-and-ready rule was that each village or group of villages had to provide enough to satisfy the royal household for 24 hours. A surviving document records that the settlement of Westbury-on-Trym, in Gloucestershire, had to supply King Offa of Mercia with seven oxen, six wethers, 40 cheeses, two tuns of clear ale, one 'cumb' full of mild ale, one 'cumb' of british ale, four 'ambers' of mead and 30 'ambers' of rye. This imposition was on a village of 60 hides—a hide being a measure of the amount of land needed by a family or that a family could conveniently cultivate in a year.

The picture we form, therefore, is of communities of industrious peasants in their lowland villages, preoccupied with wresting a living from the soil. Politically they were units in petty kingdoms some of which were no larger than a modern county. There were few towns and, in the early days, a barter economy rather than money prevailed. The king and his retainers moved from place to place administering justice, policing the countryside and collecting the royal dues.

Somewhat later, the system of 'hundreds' evolved, doubtless from an ancient custom of popular assembly, held in the open air. The term 'hundred' is thought to have referred to 100 hides, and therefore to 100 family-units, but it seems to have been used with considerable elasticity. From the king's point of view, the system took some of the burden of dispensing justice off his hands. From the viewpoint of the people, it did much to preserve their independence; at the hundred-meeting it was they who administered justice according to their age-old customs. They were responsible for the beginnings of English common law.

In addition to providing for the alimentary needs of the king and his household, the Anglo-Saxon villagers had two other major duties to the state. They had to keep the local bridges in repair and, at a later stage, they had to build and maintain local fortresses to serve as refuges in time of war (but with this we deal in a later chapter).

The significance of this background from the point of view of our theme is that the villagers who lived in these communities were those whom the warrior kings were pledged to defend and who led them into battle. Their quality, as men and as soldiers, is of obvious importance to our story. To what extent could they be relied on, and how were they organised for war? We may be sure that in many minor wars and expeditions the king's companions with their retinues were sufficient for the purpose. When, however, the nation was menaced by a large-scale invasion by the Northmen it was natural that every man would want to fight in defence of his home, his land and his family. The war against the Danes was a people's war.

Organisation, however, was necessary, and this was accomplished through the 'fyrd'. Just how this was raised and trained is not known, but it seems to have been a local levy, probably on a shire basis, for we read that the levies of Somerset, Wiltshire and west Hampshire met King Alfred somewhere in Selwood Forest prior to the battle of Ethandune. Calling out the fyrd seems to have been attended by at least two major problems. One was the difficulty of dealing with large numbers of ill-armed, ill-disciplined peasants. This was evidently recognised by some kings, for at the end of the eighth century King Cenwulf of Mercia decreed that a certain estate of 30 hides should be required to furnish only five men for the fyrd. In a citizen's army with every man called up, the number would presumably have been 30. The king evidently preferred five well-trained and well-armed men to six times that number of indifferent soldiers.

The other and even more intransigeant problem had its foundation in the fact that these were peasants; their main preoccupation was with their land. The fields had to be tilled, the seed sown, the harvest gathered, the sheep shorn and milked, the surplus cattle and pigs slaughtered and salted down for winter use. Because the cycle of the seasons governed their lives, the fyrd could never be relied upon to hold together for long. They would assemble for a battle, but they could not sustain a long campaign. Before long they would want to go home, to attend to affairs there; and they were unwilling to serve far from their own hearths. This difficulty, too, could be overcome to some extent by a selective call-up. The five men mentioned in the example given above would be happier to stay in the army for as long as they were needed if they knew that 25 neighbours back at home were seeing that their little farms did not suffer.

Approximately 300 years elapsed from the large-scale settlement of Britain by the Anglo-Saxons to the beginning of the ordeal at the hands of the Danes. It was a long time, but not long enough for the Saxon peasants to have forgotten all the warlike prowess of their fierce forefathers. Although they had become Christians they still remembered the old sagas about Beowulf, Offa and other heroes, and, of course, they found plenty of inspiration for war and battle in the stories of the Old Testament. Under the leadership of the West Saxon dynasty of warrior kings they became very effective soldiers indeed.

In the wars with the Danes the main problem of the English was to catch up with the enemy. The Danes had started their career as hit-and-run raiders, and when their forces had swollen to the status of a great army they still employed the same tactics. When they could be brought to battle the contest was, in general, a simple straightforward slogging match. The nobles dismounted and formed a shield wall, as at the Battle of Hastings.

The traditional weapon of the early Saxons was the seax or scramasax, from which they derived their name. A typical scramasax was about 18 in. long and was used dagger-fashion rather than as a sword. The Saxons were, literally, 'the men of the long knives'. There is one documentary reference to such a knife being 'smeared with poison'. By the time of the Danish wars the scramasax had been relegated to the status of an auxiliary weapon, if that, and the rank-and-file infantry relied primarily on the spear. Large numbers of Saxon spear-heads have been found in graves. Some are long, tapering, bayonet-shaped weapons, with a lozenge-shaped cross-section, while others are thinner and leaf-shaped. Some are two feet long; some only a few inches: most have a socket to fit over the wooden shaft. A complete spear (found in a grave of the period in Germany) was seven ft. long—a length which corresponds with those depicted in manuscripts.

The other common weapon of the Anglo-Saxon foot-soldier was the shield. This was normally round and made of wood (linden-wood is

specified in some Anglo-Saxon poems), with an iron boss. Some controversy exists as to whether they were convex or flat; it would seem
reasonable to suppose that the early ones were flat and that curved
surfaces were developed later. Some were beautifully made and decorated,
and many may have been bound with leather. On the whole, they were
thin (not more than about ½ in.) and light, which made them easy to
manipulate in battle. The iron boss was often pointed, thus making it a
potential weapon of offence in close fighting. The Bayeux Tapestry
depicts the Normans using kite-shaped shields, but these were not a
normal part of the Anglo-Saxon armoury. The shield-wall, referred to in
ancient poems, was probably not a barrier of interlocking shields, like the
testudo of the Roman world, but a line of warriors brandishing their light
shields, behind which they thrust at their enemies with spears and swords
or assailed them with arrows, javelins and throwing-axes.

Concerning the use of arrows, there is conflicting evidence. A poem
referring to a hail of arrows 'like sleet', has already been mentioned
(page 30), but few bows and arrows have been found in Saxon graves, and
most of those have been of indifferent quality. We know, of course, that
arrows were used by both sides at the Battle of Hastings, but it is interesting
that afterwards William the Conqueror criticised the English archers for their
poor performance. Bows and arrows were evidently poor men's weapons.

The sword, on the contrary, was a noble weapon. Usually between two
and three ft long, a thane's sword of the Viking period was a beautifully-
made weapon, double-edged, weighty and springy. The pommel and
sometimes the upper part of the blade were often elaborately decorated,
occasionally with inlaid or overlaid silver, and it seems that the scabbards
were equally ornamental. A sword was a prized possession, handed down
through generations. Often it was given a name, and minstrels sang of its
exploits in the halls on winter nights.

Javelins, or light spears which could be either used for hand-to-hand
fighting or thrown at the enemy, were weapons in use on the Continent at
this period, but few have been found in England. Another Continental
weapon occasionally though not often employed in England was the
francisca, or throwing axe. Much more frequent was the battle-axe, which
features so prominently on the Bayeux Tapestry. It was, however, a late
addition to the English armoury, having probably been adopted from the
Danes. At the lowest level were peasants armed with clubs and stones
attached to sticks, and these too are known to have operated at the Battle
of Hastings. They may, however, have not been part of the regular army
but peasants seeking revenge on soldiers who had been ravaging their
farmsteads, as the Normans undoubtedly did.

The foot-soldiers, of course, wore no uniform. Their normal garments, in peace and in war, consisted of a short tunic, a combination of trousers and stockings, cross-gartered, and a cloak fastened at the shoulder. Shoes, if worn, were buckled across the feet. Some men went bare-legged and perhaps barefoot. Richer warriors had a similar basic costume, though perhaps linen undergarments were also worn. The commonest fabric was wool, a commodity in which England was already building up an export trade in the eighth century. Spinning was a home industry, and most Anglo-Saxon huts so far excavated have produced loom-weights. Flax was also extensively grown, so linen must have been available in reasonable quantities, at least to the wealthier classes. Probably some soldiers had their tunics reinforced with leather or possibly with quilting or padding.

Common soldiers seem to have worn Phrygian caps or similar headgear, and probably these were often reinforced or lined with metal. Helmets were the prerogative of the nobles. An early helmet found in Derbyshire consists of a frame, moulded to the shape of the head, of flat iron bands into which horn plates were once fitted. It has a nose-piece (decorated in silver) and a crest. The Sutton Hoo burial mound, which was probably the cenotaph of a seventh-century king of East Anglia, has yielded an elaborately fabricated helmet which has not only a nose-piece and ear-flaps but a covering for the entire face, with holes for the eyes. This, however, was a royal helmet, and helmets were apparently not in general use until about the eleventh century. For the year 1008 *The Anglo-Saxon Chronicle* notes that it was made statutory for 'a man with eight hides only, to provide a helmet and breastplate'. By the time of the Battle of Hastings the Bayeux Tapestry depicts the knights of both sides wearing conical helmets with nose-pieces.

The Tapestry also shows knights clad in chain-mail, a form of protection which by that time was evidently in common use. It has a respectable antiquity in Anglo-Saxondom, for fragments of chain-mail were found in the seventh-century hoard at Sutton Hoo. In the fight at Maldon (Essex) between Earl Byrhtnoth and Danish invaders in 991, an Anglo-Saxon poem relates how the Earl struck a Viking 'so that his corselet burst and he was wounded in the breast through the chain mail'. A shirt of chain-mail must, however, have been so expensive that only a nobleman could afford to possess one.

The need for large quantities of weapons and armour indicates the existence of numerous skilled metal-workers. Their work was in high repute throughout Europe, for we know that Anglo-Saxon craftsmen in metal were tempted overseas to work in craft centres in Charlemagne's empire and in Rome itself.

III

Egbert

An ominous entry for the year A.D. 787 occurs in *The Anglo-Saxon Chronicle*:

This year King Beorhtric took Edburga the daughter of Offa to wife. And in his days came first three ships of the Northmen from the land of robbers. The reeve then rose thereto, and would drive them to the king's town; for he knew not what they were; and there was he slain. These were the first ships of the Danish men that sought the land of the English nation.

William of Malmesbury provides the additional information that

this band came over expressly to ascertain the fruitfulness of the soil and the courage of the inhabitants . . . Landing then, unexpectedly, when the kingdom was in a state of profound peace, they seized upon a royal village, which was nearest them, and killed the superintendant . . . but, losing their booty, through fear of the people who hastened to attack them, they retired to their ships.

A few years later *The Annals of the Britons*, which records events from the Welsh viewpoints, notes for 795, 'the first coming of the gentiles to Ireland'. The 'gentiles' or 'the black gentiles' are terms used by the British chroniclers for the Danes.

A new enemy had appeared on the English scene.

The reference to the 'profound peace' that prevailed in the latter half of the eighth century is confirmed by a perusal of *The Anglo-Saxon Chronicle*. From the year 754, when the warlike West Saxon king Cuthred died, to 793 it contains no records of any wars between Saxon kingdoms, though the Mercian king, Offa, conducted one or two campaigns against the Welsh. 793 was the year of the first Danish attacks on Northumbria, beginning with the assault on Holy Isle, but until the end of the century the rest of England was left in tranquillity.

The period was, indeed, one of comparative peace and prosperity for the whole of western Europe. It was the age of Charlemagne, the great Frankish emperor—a golden age which medieval troubadours viewed through the rose-tinted spectacles of romance but which did indeed see most of the former provinces of the Roman Empire again temporarily united under one ruler. Charlemagne's Holy Roman Empire embraced most of modern France, Germany, Italy, Switzerland, Austria and the Netherlands, together with a slice of Spain, while in the forests and plains beyond the eastern frontier great areas of what are now Yugoslavia, Hungary, Czechoslovakia and Poland were tributary.

In 732 Charles Martel, the Frankish general who was Charlemagne's grandfather, had defeated the Moslem armies at Tours, one of the decisive battles of the world. His son, Pepin, deposed the last of the degenerate Mcrovingian kings and was accepted as king of the Franks. To this realm Pepin's son, Charlemagne, succeeded in 768. Charlemagne spent the first ten years of his reign in consolidating his kingdom against rebellious provinces and family rivals. By 778 he felt strong enough to mount a campaign against the Moslems of Spain which, although not at first successful, eventually resulted in the establishment of a new province, the Spanish March. He crossed the Alps, annexed the kingdom of the Lombards and occupied Rome. The rest of his long reign witnessed a series of campaigns in the east, many of them against the still heathen Saxons who lived in the valleys of the lower Elbe and Weser. He also had to contend with one of those periodic irruptions of nomadic horsemen from the steppes of Asia into central Europe. These savages, the Avars, against whom he waged incessant war for seven years, were eventually overcome and virtually exterminated.

On Christmas Day, in the year 800, Charlemagne summoned his vassals and retainers to Rome to his coronation. He had intended to crown himself but the Pope, Leo III, seized the crown at the critical moment and placed it on Charlemagne's head. Thereafter the new empire was known as the Holy Roman Empire, and popes claimed the right to crown its emperors.

In spite of this disturbing little episode, Charlemagne set great value on the co-operation of the Church. Although himself highly intelligent and a student of, among other subjects, Latin, Greek, arithmetic and astronomy, he could not read or write, though he tried hard at times to master the art of letters. To run his vast empire he needed the help of literate men, whom he could find only within the Church. Among his chief assistants was Alcuin, an Englishman from York and one of the leading scholars of his age. When returning from a pilgrimage to Rome in 781 he met Charlemagne, who offered him charge of the palace school at Aachen. There Alcuin lived for many years, on terms of personal friendship with Charlemagne, whom he advised on both church and secular matters. Many other English scholars came to join him at Charlemagne's court.

This was only one aspect of the increasingly close links between the Anglo-Saxon kingdoms and the Continent. Offa of Mercia, who was undisputedly supreme among the English kings until his death in 796, corresponded with Charlemagne on equal terms. A treaty between the two monarchs in 796 is the first trade agreement in English history. It was, in fact, made to regulate a resumption of commerce after an interruption due to a mild quarrel between Charlemagne and Offa, back in 789. Charlemagne had suggested that his son should marry one of Offa's daughters. To this Offa had agreed, provided that one of Charlemagne's daughters married his son, Ecgfrith, but on that point negotiations broke down, for Charlemagne idolised his daughters to such an extent that he couldn't bear to part with them. They had love-affairs and bore illegitimate children with impunity, but he couldn't bring himself to let them marry and leave home.

This digression into Continental affairs at the court of Charlemagne has considerable relevance to our story, for it was at that court that Egbert received his training. To explain how he came to be there *The Anglo-Saxon Chronicle* relates the following story in commendable detail. In 754 the West Saxon king, Cuthred, who engaged in frequent wars with Mercia, died and was succeeded by an unworthy relative named Sebright. After a year, the West Saxon Witan, or Council, displeased with Sebright's misbehaviour, authorised another member of the royal family, Cynewulf, to take over. Sebright was driven into exile and soon afterwards killed.

Nearly 30 years later (and the time-lapse demonstrates the strength of blood-feuds in those days) a kinsman of Sebright named Cyneard saw a chance of avenging Sebright's death: 'He, having understood that the king was gone, thinly attended, on a visit to a lady at Merton, rode after him and beset him therein; surrounding the town without, ere the attendants of the king were aware of him.' A fierce fight ensued in which as many of the king's bodyguard who heard the noise rushed to join, but both they and the king were killed. Next day an avenging party arrived. Cyneard tried to bribe them to accept him as king, but they refused and eventually managed to force the gates and settle accounts with the assassins. 'Eighty-four men', besides Cyneard, says *The Chronicle*, were killed.

As a result of this affray, the royal house of Wessex was somewhat depleted. The choice of the next king apparently lay between one Beorhtric and Egbert. Egbert was the great-grandson of Ingild, King Ina's brother, and son of a man named Elmund, who was under-king of Kent, presumably subject to Wessex. William of Malmesbury says that Egbert was 'a daring and ambitious young man', who considered he had best right to the crown. The choice of the Council, however, was Beorhtric. They had evidently had enough of violence and bloodshed, and they rightly judged Beorhtric to be a man of peace. William of Malmesbury describes him as 'skilful in conciliating friendship, affable with foreigners, and giving great allowances to his subjects, in those matters at least which could not impair the strength of the government.'

He reigned in tranquillity for 16 years.

At the beginning of his reign, however, he rightly saw a dangerous rival in Egbert, who prudently removed himself to the court of Mercia. Learning where he was, Beorhtric sent a delegation to King Offa, ostensibly to arrange a marriage between Beorhtric and Offa's daughter, Edburga, but also, privately, to offer a bribe to have Egbert returned to Wessex. Egbert, learning that Offa was likely to yield, went on his travels again, this time to the court of Charlemagne, where he remained till Beorhtric's death.

Up to this time Egbert, in the opinion of William of Malmesbury, was, although ambitious, affected by 'the rust of indolence', but his experiences in Aachen toughened him. He was there, evidently, for the 16 years that Beorhtric reigned in Wessex and therefore during many of the almost incessant campaigns of Charlemagne. At first-hand he was able to study the administration of a great empire, the conduct of wars against formidable foes and the military tactics devised by a soldier of genius, as well as to enjoy life at the most brilliant and luxurious court in the western world.

Whether he attended Charlemagne's coronation on Christmas Day of the year 800, however, is doubtful, for in that same year he was called back to Wessex for his own coronation. King Beorhtric had died of poison administered by his wife. Apparently she had been accustomed to dominate an easy-going husband but then realised that he was neglecting her advice and company, preferring instead that of a young ealderman named Warr. She forthwith set about poisoning the young man, which she did successfully, but unfortunately the king also drank the same concoction.

This time Egbert had no real rival in Wessex. On the invitation of the Witan he returned and was crowned in 800 A.D. His accession was marked by a minor invasion of Wessex by an opportunist ealderman, Ethelmund, of the Hwicce, a people who lived by the Severn in the modern Worcestershire. Says *The Anglo-Saxon Chronicle*,

He rode over the Thames at Kempsford; where he was met by Alderman Woxtan, with the men of Wiltshire, and a terrible conflict ensued, in which

both commanders were slain, but the men of Wiltshire obtained the
victory.

Egbert himself took no part in this battle, which occurred on 'the same
day' as either his accession or his coronation—it is not stated which. The
trouncing which the Hwicce received seems to have discouraged anyone
else who might have had similar ideas, and thereafter for at least a decade
Wessex was left in peace. The new king of Mercia, Ceolwulf, took control
however of Sussex, Kent, Essex and East Anglia as well as his own kingdom, and Egbert was for a time content to let him do so unchallenged.

There is little doubt that, from the very beginning of his reign, Egbert
had set his sights on becoming ruler of all Britain, or as much of it as
possible. As already noted, he was ambitious, and at Charlemagne's court
he had studied how an empire was forged and welded out of a number of
formerly independent units. One can almost see him forming the resolu-
tion that what Charlemagne had done in western Europe he would do in
the new state that would be called England. But such lofty goals are not
attained without careful preparation, and Egbert was content to wait till
he was ready. Meantime, he doubtless set about organising his army on
Continental lines, though we have no information about the innovations
he introduced. Possibly, like Arthur before him, he imported heavier
breeds of horses than the native ponies. Cavalry played an important role
in Charlemagne's victories, especially against the Avars, and it is noteworthy that when Egbert began his wars in England he was able to move
about the country at a smart pace.

While we can be sure that it was Egbert who forged the weapon which
enabled his grandson, Alfred, to meet and turn the Danish tide, it was not
against the Danes that Egbert used it, at least until the closing years of
his reign. His first campaign was against the Britons of what remained of
the old kingdom of Dyvnaint, which now coincided more or less with
Cornwall. *The Chronicle* records that in 813 he 'spread devastation in
Cornwall from east to west'. William of Malmesbury says that he 'sub-
jugated' the Britons who lived there, but it must have been an uneasy
conquest, for ten years later we read of a battle at 'Gafulford' between the
'Wala and Defna'. The 'Wala' are held to be the Britons (Welsh), the
'Defna' the people of Devonshire, and 'Gafulford' has been tentatively
identified as Camelford.

Perhaps taking advantage of Egbert's absence in the south-western
peninsula the king of Mercia, in an ill-advised moment, chose to attack
Wessex. Beornwulf, the Mercian king, was a newcomer, having succeeded
to the throne in that same year, 823. Probably he needed an inexpensive
victory, for he had taken over the kingdom by deposing his predecessor,

Ceolwulf, who had won a considerable reputation by a victorious campaign against the Welsh, which had resulted in the capture of their fortress, Deganwy, and the virtual annexation of the kingdom of Powys.

Beornwulf at the head of a formidable army entered Wessex. The wording of William of Malmesbury's account suggests that he achieved a limited surprise over Egbert who, however, 'deeming it disgraceful to retreat, met him with much spirit'. The result was a resounding defeat for the Mercians at the Battle of Ellendun, which has been variously identified as Wilton, Allington near Salisbury, and several other places, but which is now thought to be a locality on the downs near Wroughton, which would place it very near Arthur's celebrated battle of Mount Badon. (There is a modern Ellendune housing estate at Wroughton.)

One thing Egbert had learned at Aachen was to strike while the iron was hot. Giving the Mercians no chance to recover, he sent his son Ethelwulf, accompanied by the Bishop of Sherborne, an ealderman named Wulfherd and a large army straight over to Kent to demand submission. This errand they successfully achieved, collecting the allegiance of Sussex, Surrey and Essex at the same time. The king of East Anglia, in rebellion against the Mercians, also asked for and received assistance. In fighting against the East Angles later in the year the unlucky Beornwulf was killed, and the power of Mercia collapsed for ever. It was a great year for Egbert. With a series of hammer-blows he had become master of all the south of Britain from Land's End to Thanet, with other Anglo-Saxon kingdoms seeking his friendship and hardly an enemy in sight.

A point that strikes us about this successful campaign is that somehow, by means not recorded, Egbert had built up an army prepared to serve outside its native shires and to stay in the field for considerable periods. That alone was a notable achievement.

There followed a hiatus of four years. Then in 827, Egbert struck again. This time it was a campaign, entirely successful, for the conquest of Mercia. Egbert even entitled himself, on coins, King of the Mercians. From Mercia he went on to subdue the Northumbrians, but they met him at a place named Dore, near Sheffield and offered their submission. *The Anglo-Saxon Chronicle* exultantly proclaims Egbert as the 'eighth king who was sovereign of all the British dominions', conveniently forgetting Offa, of the discredited Mercia, who had had at least as good a claim to the title.

In the following year *The Chronicle* states laconically that 'Wiglaf obtained again the Mercian kingdom'. Wiglaf had been deposed by Egbert and students of the period are at a loss to know whether he was reinstated as a subject-king or whether he led a successful revolt. William of Malmesbury accepts the first alternative and it certainly seems the more likely, for in the same year Egbert 'led an army against the people of North Wales and compelled them all to peaceful submission.' He could hardly have reached North Wales without crossing Mercian territory and would have been unlikely to embark on a campaign against the Welsh with Mercia in revolt behind his back. However, whether independent or a subject state of Wessex, Mercia is known from charters to have held land south of the Thames, in Berkshire, until at least as late as 844, and London remained a Mercian city until it was taken over by the Danes.

Egbert's later years were clouded by the growing menace of the Danes. In 833, 35 Danish ships landed at Charmouth, in Dorset. We can imagine Egbert, informed of the intrusion, galloping with his companions post-haste to the coast and collecting what levies he could *en route* to attack the raiders. William of Malmesbury preserves the fullest account of the battle. He says,

When, during the greater part of the day, he had almost secured the victory, he lost the battle as the sun declined; however, by the favour of darkness, he escaped the disgrace of being conquered.

The Anglo-Saxon Chronicle records that a great slaughter was made but that the Danes remained masters of the field. Other sources comment that after this defeat Egbert called a council of his nobles to consider means of strengthening the defences of the kingdom.

The next test came in 835, when the Danes combined with the Britons in Cornwall to stir up trouble in the far west. *The Anglo-Saxon Chronicle* refers to this as a full-scale war, saying that the Danes came with a great fleet and were joined by the Cornish people. This time Egbert seems to have arrived on the scene better prepared, having probably taken more time to collect an adequate army. He met the combined forces of the Britons and Danes at Hingston Down, near Callington—a height just to the west of the Tamar—and won a resounding victory. His triumph was still remembered, a source of pride and hope, 40 years later by West Saxons grown weary from continual defeats.

After the battle of Hingston Down the Danes doubtless escaped by sea, for two years later a fleet of about the same number of ships raided Southampton, and three years after that they were at Charmouth again. But by then Egbert was dead. He died in 837, having reigned for 37 years. His age is not known, but as he spent approximately 16 years at the court of Charlemagne and as he was regarded as a promising young man, probably aged twenty or more, when he went there he must have been in his seventies, which was a good age for those troubled times. There was evidently nothing on his side of the family to account for the distressing physical weakness which afflicted so many of his descendants.

Among his last acts had been the pacification of Cornwall. He severely punished them, say the records, and threatened the Britons throughout the whole kingdom of Wessex with extermination if he had any more trouble. He would have been capable of carrying out the threat, for in Old Saxony he had participated in Charlemagne's campaigns against a recalcitrant people and knew about, even if he did not witness, the occasion when Charlemagne had 4,500 Saxon prisoners beheaded in one day.

Egbert was a stern and ruthless man. He needed to be.

IV

The Enemy

'From the fury of the Northmen, O Lord, deliver us,' chanted the ninth-century monks of western Europe, with good reason, for they had been entirely unprepared for the horror which burst upon them. To the Dorset reeve who was killed when he challenged the crews of the three ships that landed near Dorchester in 787 the newcomers were quite unfamiliar. If he had had any suspicion of what to expect he would have been more cautious.

Six years later the unprovoked attack on the highly respected and defenceless monastic community of Lindisfarne horrified western Christendom. Afterwards the compilers of *The Anglo-Saxon Chronicle* remembered that

this year came dreadful fore-warnings over the land of the Northumbrians, terrifying the people most woefully; these were immense sheets of light rushing through the air, and whirlwinds, and fiery dragons flying across the firmament. These tremendous tokens were soon followed by a great famine. . . .

There were rumours, too, of drops of blood having been seen to fall from the roof of St. Peter's Church, York.

Alcuin, the great English scholar at the Frankish court, when he heard the news of the raid attributed it to divine retribution on the Northumbrians for their sins. There had, in fact, been one or two assassinations of Northumbrian royalty over the previous year. It was, however, a premature judgement by Alcuin, for the tempest, of which this was the first ominous forerunner, was to spread devastation not only over Northumbria and every other English kingdom but over every country in western Europe, from Ireland and northern France down to and including the countries of the western Mediterranean. But no-one could possibly have foreseen the extent and severity of the catastrophe.

45

In a previous chapter we noted a contemporary reference to the profound peace which prevailed in much of England in the last quarter of the eighth century A.D. The peace extended to most of Europe, now largely united under the strong but tolerant rule of Charlemagne. Such wars as occurred were being waged along the frontiers of the new Roman Empire, as in northern Spain and Old Saxony. Away from these border zones the arts and commerce of peace flourished. Agriculture prospered, towns were being established as trade developed, merchants travelled freely from country to country, in convents and monasteries exquisite art treasures were being produced. The civilization of old Rome was being revived in a renaissance which, unfortunately, proved to be a false dawn.

The reasons for the Nordic invasions of the ninth to eleventh centuries are not so much obscure as complex. Although in many respects the irruption was similar to that of the Anglo-Saxons several hundreds of years earlier, some of the elements were lacking. In particular, the Danes and Norwegians did not have the excuse of being under pressure from other enemies; nobody was pushing them from behind. Nor could they cite crop-failure due to a change in climate, such as has often triggered off folk-migrations, for the eighth to eleventh centuries seem to have been blessed with a rather warmer and more stable climate than the northern countries enjoy at present. Moreover, it was only in the later phases of the conflict that the Nordic peoples thought about migration and colonisation. Earlier the raiders were simple robbers, bent on seizing as much loot as they could and going home with it before vengeance overtook them.

Nevertheless it does seem likely that the northern countries were overpopulated. Thousands of them fell in battle, according to the chronicles, and still they came, 'like swarms of grasshoppers, like endless ocean waves'. One reason for this surplus of young men was that the Northmen were polygamous. They had as many wives as they could afford and as many concubines as they could acquire, and they took a pride in siring as many sons as possible. This may have been all very well for the father, but when the time came for the next generation to take over quarrels were inevitable. For every son who succeeded in consolidating the ancestral inheritance there must have been a horde of brothers whose best hope of survival lay in making themselves scarce. So off they went to seek their fortunes elsewhere.

A word here about the several terms applied to the Northmen will not be out-of-place. *The Anglo-Saxon Chronicle* calls them first the heathen, then the Danes. Frankish records refer to them as the *Normanin*, or Northmen. Irish and Welsh chronicles dub them 'foreigners', 'strangers' and 'gentiles', sometimes differentiating between the 'black' and the 'white' gentiles. The black ones were evidently the Danes, the white the Norwegians, and the colour adjectives are thought to have referred to their clothes or their shields. In German records they are the *Ascomanni* or 'Ashmen', perhaps because the hafts of their spears were of ash, perhaps because they venerated that tree. Finally, there was the more general term, the Vikings, about the origin and meaning of which controversy has raged. According to one school of thought, the word is derived from 'vik', a creek; according to another, from 'wic', a camp or fortified settlement; there are other suggested derivations. Viking is a useful term for it can be used to describe Danes, Norwegians or Swedes, when it is uncertain which nation the pirates belonged to. From the point of view of our story, however, it is clear that the earlier invaders of England were predominantly, though not exclusively, Danes.

The first of the Nordic peoples to go on the rampage were the Swedes. That fact has considerable significance in the context of what followed. It was natural, for geographical reasons, for the Swedes to go east, and already by the early eighth century, nearly 100 years before the Viking menace became apparent in England, they had crossed the Baltic and were expanding into what is now Russia. In the years that followed they spread their influence gradually southwards and eastwards, establishing first trading-posts and then towns. Among their most important centres were Old Ladoga, Novgorod and later, Kiev. At Kiev they were on the southward flowing Dnieper down which they could travel to the Black Sea. Beyond lay two of the wealthiest and most civilised states of the world, Byzantium (or Constantinople) and Baghdad, the capital of the Arab caliph, Haroun al Rashid.

The Swedes were primarily traders. They raided and squabbled and established independent kingdoms en route, but their main motive was the age-old one of 'making a fast buck'. Writes an Arab observer,

They have no cultivated fields but depend for their supplies on what they can get from the Slavs (who were living in these parts). When a son is born the father advances on the baby, sword in hand, and flings it down, saying, 'I shall not leave you any property; you have only what you can provide with this weapon.'

He adds that they are brave in battle but fight best from ships. They are unreliable and perfidious, 'even a man's brother or comrade is not above plundering him if he can'.

Another Arab, quoting from personal observation, supplies the words of a prayer offered by a Swede to his idol before embarking on an expedition to an Arab market:

O Lord, I have come from distant parts with so many girls, so many sable furs (and whatever other commodities are in his catalogue). I now bring you this offering. Please send me a merchant who has many dinars and dirhams and who will trade favourably with me without contradicting me.

The optimistic dream of every trader through the ages.

The relevance of all this is that here lay the prime market which the raiders in the west were aiming to supply. No doubt large quantities of gold, jewels and valuable personal belongings looted from western halls and monasteries were retained in Denmark, Norway or wherever they were taken at the end of a raid, but many other items, especially slaves, were passed on to traders who dealt with the fabulous East. Many a flaxen-haired Anglo-Saxon girl, kidnapped from her home in Northumbria, Kent, Wessex or elsewhere, must eventually have found herself in a slave-market in Baghdad, en route to an oriental harem.

Although enjoying a fight, therefore, and worshipping the virile and savage gods of the North—Odin, Thor, Tyr, Balder and the rest—the early raiders of the West were not battle-hungry; they much preferred the hit-and-run raid. If they could get what they wanted without fighting, they did. Time and again in the Anglo-Saxon records we read of shiploads of Danes eluding the forces sent to intercept them. The main problem of the Anglo-Saxons was not so much to defeat the enemy in battle but to corner them so that they had to fight. And here the English, like the Romanised Britons before them, were at an enormous disadvantage. Theirs was no narrow frontier to defend but a vast, indented coastline, stretching from the Firth of Forth to the Bristol Channel. Whatever may have been the population of England in those days, it was inadequate for such a task. The system of local levies was probably the best that could be devised, but as often as not by the time the local thane had collected his men and rode to intercept the raiders, the latter had dashed back to their ships with their booty and were standing away out to sea. It was only later, when the Danes had embarked on a programme of conquest and colonisation and were land-based in England, that the English armies could meet them on more equal terms.

Until King Alfred began the construction of an English navy, no real attempt was apparently made to meet the Northmen on their own element, the sea. Such an attempt, if it had been made in the early days, would have been doomed to failure for the Anglo-Saxon ships were no match for the superb vessels of the Danes. Although one or two English poems refer to ships with sails, only one Anglo-Saxon ship has been discovered and it has no sails. Propulsion may well have been mainly by oars. The Viking ships, on the other hand, bore great sails fastened to a central mast. They were constructed of overlapping planking and, unlike many older types of vessel, possessed a strong keel. Of three almost complete Viking ships which have been excavated in Norway, the best known is the Gokstad ship, 70 ft. long and made of oak, and dating from around 900 A.D. In a facsimile of this ship a successful crossing of the Atlantic was made in 1893, under a Norwegian captain who spoke highly of its seaworthiness. And, of course, in such ships Viking colonists as well as raiders navigated the stormy ocean to Iceland, Greenland and the mysterious Vinland which must have been somewhere in North America.

Such was the main asset of the Viking raiders who afflicted England throughout the ninth century. It goes almost without saying that the Northmen were superb sailors who knew well how to handle their ships. In war they used the conventional weapons, chiefly swords, spears and arrows but with the addition of one of their own, the battle-axe. Most pictures of Vikings depict them swinging a huge battle-axe with concave blade. A formidable weapon it must have been, but nevertheless it takes time to swing an axe, and while it was raised above his head, the axe-man would have been highly vulnerable to a swordsman with sufficient courage to venture beneath his guard. As with the Anglo-Saxons, early shields were round, the kite-shaped ones depicted in the Bayeux Tapestry belonging to a later phase. Like other warriors of their age, the Vikings had coats of chain-mail and helmets which were either of iron or of leather reinforced with iron.

Unlike many seafaring peoples, the Vikings were good horsemen and, in fact, thought highly of their horses. When in the later raids on England they grew bolder and ventured far inland, almost invariably their first preoccupation on disembarking was to provide themselves with horses. Their consequent mobility on land was as alarming to the English as their mastery of the sea.

While one factor in triggering off the Viking raids was undoubtedly the opening of the markets of the East by the Swedes, another was, parodoxically, the success of Charlemagne in reviving the Roman Empire. His long campaigns in the north of his vast realm eventually resulted in the virtual elimination of the Saxons of Old Saxony, a process which brought him face-to-face with the next kingdom to the north, that of the Danes.

Denmark at that time had become a united kingdom, comprising Jutland, the Danish islands and probably part of Scania, on the Swedish mainland. Its king, Godfred, claimed to have some kind of overlordship over both Frisia and Old Saxony, so in his campaigns Charlemagne was theoretically encroaching on his territory. It took no great perspicacity on Godfred's part to see himself as next on the list so, in anticipation of trouble, he caused a prodigious earthwork, the Danevirke, to be constructed across the base of the Danish peninsula. A probable war between Godfred and Charlemagne was averted by the murder of Godfred in the year 810, and a long civil war between his would-be successors removed the Danish threat for a time, as far as Charlemagne was concerned.

The confrontation did mean, however, that for the first time the Danes and a revived Roman world could take a good look at each other at close quarters. Superficially, this was all to the good. There were diplomatic exchanges, and missions, and trade. Horik, who managed to secure control of the Danish realm in 825 and who reigned as king till 854, strove hard to keep the peace with the Empire. He maintained throughout his reign diplomatic contact with Louis the Pious, who succeeded his father Charlemagne in 814, and gave a safe conduct to a Christian missionary, St. Anskar, whom Louis sent to introduce Christianity to the North. So far events followed the usual pattern of development between the Roman Empire and barbarian nations.

But Horik had an ulterior motive in his efforts to keep the peace. Among those who displayed an enthusiastic interest in the civilised world now on their doorstep were the restless young hooligans who were being spawned in embarrassing numbers. Until the subjugation of Old Saxony the Saxons and Friesians had dominated the North Sea, imposing a barrier between the Nordic heathens and the civilised lands to the West. Now that barrier was removed, and the pirate crews of Denmark were able to assess both the wealth and the weakness of the West. To the East these young men were in contact with an insatiable market for commodities —notably slaves, which they now discovered could be had for the taking. The Danes were born traders, and here was a golden opportunity to get rich quick. This, naturally, did not suit Horik. If anyone was going to benefit from this new traffic it must be himself, not these irreverent and independent young men. Their presence back in Denmark, swaggering around with their newly-acquired riches, was a menace to his authority. He tried hard to keep them under control and succeeded for nearly 30 years, but at last he met the fate of so many ninth-century kings. He was assassinated and almost his entire family wiped out.

The Danish kingdom then disintegrated into warring clans and, with anarchy at home, the Vikings went plundering abroad just as they pleased. As the Bible records of a similar situation in old Israel: 'In those days there was no king, but every man did that which was right in his own eyes.'

The early raids seem to have been entirely co-operative efforts. A Viking ship sailing up the river Eure, in France, was challenged by a Frankish herald who demanded, 'Who is your master?'

'None. We are all equals,' was the inspiring reply of the Vikings. One of the earliest Viking ships excavated in Denmark, at Ladby, had no special place for a leader. All took a hand at the oars. But this democratic arrangement must have soon been modified. *The Anglo-Saxon Chronicle* records that in 833, three years before his death, King Egbert fought with 35 pirate ships at Charmouth: 'A great slaughter was made, and the Danes remained masters of the field'. This encounter has already been described, but a salient fact is that here were 35 shiploads of Danes working together. Discipline, organisation and an accepted leader are implied.

Again, in 835 when Egbert won his important victory over the combined forces of the Danes and the Britons at Hingston Down, *The Chronicle* states that the Danes arrived in a great fleet. By 837, the year after Egbert's death, the Danes who fought at Portland were described by *The Chronicle* as 'the army' or 'the host'; in 851 'three hundred and fifty ships came into the mouth of the Thames'. The raids became more formidable year by year. Nor were they confined to the English side of the English Channel. England, Frankland, were all the same to the pirates. If they met with opposition in one locality they moved on to another where the pickings were easier. While Egbert was still alive and providing a check on their inroads, they poured into France, sailing up the Seine to attack Paris and up the Loire to Nantes. A Frankish chronicle recites the catalogue of destruction:

They seize Bordeaux, Perigueux, Limoges, Angouleme, Toulouse; Angers, Tours and Orleans are made deserts . . . everywhere Christ's people are the victims of massacre. . . .

After the death of Louis the Pious in 840 the Empire of Charlemagne broke up, being divided between Louis's three sons. Charles, nicknamed the Bald, took what is now France; Ludwig had Germany; and Lothar reigned over a central sector named after him Lotharingia, the name now surviving in Lorraine. Little friendship existed between the brothers, and once, in the 860s, when Charles and Lothar united in an attempt to clear out an enclave of Vikings who had established themselves in an island in the Seine, Ludwig took advantage of the situation to invade France from the rear. It was during this campaign that an incident occurs which throws a vivid light on the Viking character. While the Frankish armies were still besieging the island, named Jeufosse, another Danish horde arrived, 200 ships under the command of a Viking named Weland, and offered to help the Franks in return for a huge bribe—5,000 pounds of silver and all the provisions they needed. The Vikings would do virtually anything for a profit.

Another nation, scarcely mentioned yet in this story, was involved in the demonic explosion of Viking energy in the ninth, tenth and eleventh centuries. The Norwegians, Norse or Northmen had a different background from the Danes. Theirs was a mountainous land split by deep fjords, and until late in the ninth century it had no unified government. It was, however, affected, as was Denmark, by a rapidly increasing population. Its mountain pastures, hemmed in by an ice-locked plateau, offered no scope for expansion and its young men naturally took to the sea.

By the end of the eighth century their ships were roving far and wide over the northern parts of the North Sea. They cleared the Shetlands, Orkneys and some of the Hebrides of their sparse population, probably Pictish, and formed permanent settlements there. Then they moved southwestwards to Ireland. The Irish, though they had now been civilized for 3-400 years and had indeed been a haven for scholarship and Christianity during the chaos attending the collapse of the Roman Empire, were not militarily or politically equipped to deal with the challenge. Their government still resided in the hands of independent chiefs, and they had no fortified towns on which to base resistance. On the other hand, their monasteries were replete with treasure, to which the Norwegians helped themselves after butchering the monks.

Ireland's first real town was Dublin, which the Norwegian chief, Turgeis, is said to have founded in 839 after he had styled himself 'king of all the foreigners in Ireland'. He was an enthusiastic pagan who desecrated the deeply revered Christian shrine at Armagh and set up there an altar to Thor. Moreover, he was backed up by the support of a powerful fleet. Driven to desperation, the Irish eventually managed to catch him and executed him by drowning in a loch. In a typically Celtic lament, an Irish chronicler of the time mourned,

If a hundred heads of hardened iron could grow on one neck, and if each head possessed a hundred sharp tongues of tempered metal, and if each tongue cried out incessantly with a hundred ineradicable loud voices, they would never be able to enumerate the griefs which the people of Ireland— men and women, laymen and priests, young and old—have suffered at the hands of these warlike ruthless barbarians.

In 851 the Irish, on the principle that nothing could be worse than their present state, called in the Danes to help them repel the Norwegians: again we have the spectacle of two Viking peoples fighting each other. For a time, the alliance worked. The Norwegians were soundly defeated, then reinforcements arrived from Norway and the tables were turned. The Danes were chased out of Ireland (in that same year, 851), leaving the

Norwegians undisputed rulers of the country. They formed two kingdoms there, one based on Dublin, the other on Limerick.

In an earlier chapter we referred to England being exposed to Viking raids all along its coasts. It was also exposed on the west to attack from Ireland, just as in the days of the Anglo-Saxon invasion 400 years earlier, when the Irish and Picts united with the Anglo-Saxons to attack Roman Britain. The threat was there, though its implementation depended on the current degree of friendship or hostility between the Danes involved in England and the Norwegians resident in Erin. There was no guarantee that the bitter foes of one week would not be friends the next.

The assault on England was carried out mainly by the Danes in the south, with Norwegians participating farther north, particularly in Northumbria. Later the Norwegians were the predominant influence there. On the Continent the Danes apparently concentrated on the northern coast of France, which was most easily accessible from their bases in Denmark and Frisia, while the Norwegians descended on the west coast, *via* Ireland. The sack of Nantes in 843 was, it seems, a mainly Norwegian escapade. After collecting their plunder, the Norsemen established a settlement on the island of Noirmoutier at the mouth of the Loire, and proceeded to organise a protection racket, taking toll of all commerce along the Loire and the western seaboard.

Two notable Viking exploits which are peripheral to our story but which illustrate the formidable character of the enemies with which the warrior kings of Saxon England had to deal were the expeditions to the Mediterranean in 844 and 859/62. It is likely that the first one was a Norwegian enterprise, and the second one may have been, though it was led apparently by two Danes. Perhaps the crews were of mixed nationality. In 844 the ships followed the coast of western France and northern Spain to Galicia, where they attacked the town of Corunna but were repulsed. Sailing on, they had better luck at Lisbon, which they captured. Then they moved on through the Straits of Gibraltar into the Mediterranean, where they took and plundered the towns of Cadiz and Seville— no mean feat in view of the strength of the Arab state of Cordova at that time.

The expedition of 859/62 was a much larger one, consisting of no fewer than 62 ships which set out from the mouth of the Loire and worked their way southwards, looting on the Iberian coast wherever they found weak defences. Passing through the Straits of Gibraltar they sacked Algeciras and then crossed over to North Africa, where they committed their usual depredations and collected much booty, including several negroes—the first they had ever seen. Veering north, they landed in the Camargue in the south of France and stayed there for some time. In the next year, 860, they moved southwards along the coast of Italy, sacking Pisa and capturing the city of Luna, which they were deceived into thinking was Rome. According to an Arab record, they then voyaged far to the east, reaching Alexandria. When they returned home in 862, 40 of their ships had been lost, but the surviving 22 certainly had a tale to tell that occupied the attentions of their bards for many a year, and a tremendous treasure in the bargain.

V

Ethelwulf

There are remarkable parallels between the ninth-century course of events in Wessex and the Holy Roman Empire. In each case a warlike, vigorous monarch was succeeded by a son who might be regarded as excessively civilised. But in each case the son, though by some of his contemporaries considered to be pusillanimous, proved on balance to have been as successful as possible under the circumstances, and each, when forced to make war, gave a good account of himself in battle.

The European monarch was Louis the Pious, whose *soubriquet* indicates how he was regarded at the time; the West Saxon, Ethelwulf, son of that man of iron, Egbert. Of Louis Sir Frank Stenton comments,

By keeping in touch with events on the border through *missi* and local officers, by playing off one member of the Danish royal family against another, and by maintaining diplomatic relations with the man possessed of the greatest power among the Danes, Louis kept the Frankish dominions from devastation for twenty years.

The same tribute might be paid to Ethelwulf, except that in his case diplomacy and watchfulness had on several occasions to be reinforced by hard fighting. Ethelwulf was apparently Egbert's only son, by his wife Redburga. The date of his birth is not known but could have been 801, the year after Egbert's return from exile. This would make Ethelwulf twenty-four at the time of the battle of Ellendune, which would seem reasonable in view of the fact that he took part in the battle and was immediately afterwards sent to accept the allegiance of Kent and, if necessary, to enforce it.

Egbert apparently had reservations about his son and heir. The chroniclers say that Ethelwulf was unwarlike and that he leaned too heavily towards the Church. William of Malmesbury describes him as 'of heavy and sluggish disposition' and comments that 'mild by nature, he infinitely preferred a life of tranquillity to dominion over many provinces'. The same, of course, could be said of King Alfred, who much preferred peace to war, but we know what he could do when he had to. Ethelwulf may well have been a man of the same type. Whatever the truth about his character, Ethelwulf had the inestimable asset of the support of wise advisers. The two chief ones, perhaps chosen by his father, were Bishop Swithun of Winchester (afterwards St. Swithun) and Bishop Ealstan of Sherborne. They were men of completely contrasting character, in many ways complementing each other.

Ealstan was the practical character. Says William of Malmesbury,

Knowing that the business of the kingdom ought not to be neglected, he continually inspirited him against the Danes; himself furnishing the exchequer with money, as well as regulating the army.

Ealstan was evidently one of those militant prelates so frequent in the annals of the medieval church. It was he whom Egbert sent over to Kent with Ethelwulf to take charge of that kingdom after the battle of Ellendune. He doubtless considered that Ealstan would compensate for any weaknesses in the character of his son. In the later years of Ethelwulf's reign it was Ealstan who conspired with the crown prince, Ethelbald, to depose Ethelwulf, probably preferring a stronger leader to face the dangers then threatening. William of Malmesbury is in two minds about him: 'He held his bishopric fifty years,' he writes, 'happy in living for so long a space in the practice of good works'; but then he goes on, 'I should readily commend him, had he not been swayed by worldly avarice, and usurped what belonged to others.' And he reveals his prejudice by adding, 'when by his intrigues he seized the monastery of Malmesbury for his own use.'

Malmesbury was, of course, William's monastery, and even in his day, 300 years afterwards, there was evidently still a black mark against Ealstan's name in the Abbey annals. William sums it up in the sentence, 'Thus the accursed passion of avarice corrupts the human soul, and forces men, though great and illustrious in other respects, into hell.'

Ethelwulf's other counsellor, Swithun, was a man of decidedly saintly character. Several legends have attached to his name, and all testify to his humanity and humility. The well-known story of 40 days' rain following a wet St. Swithun's Day and of apples being christened on that day relate to an incident more than 100 years after his death. Swithun, who was Bishop of Winchester, had requested that his body be buried under a pathway in the cathedral churchyard so that those who entered the building would walk over the grave. When, later, he was canonised the clergy of Winchester thought it not right that so eminent a man should have such a lowly resting place, so they prepared to have the body removed, with great ceremony, to a new tomb in the choir of the cathedral on 15 July 983. But, says John Brand, in his *Observations of Popular Antiquities*,

it rained so violently on that day, and for forty days succeeding, as had hardly ever been known, which made them set aside their design as heretical and blasphemous, and, instead, they erected a chapel over his grave, at which many miracles are said to have been wrought.

Another episode which throws a favourable light on Swithun's character is encapsulated in the following seventeenth-century rhyme:

A woman having broke her eggs
By stumbling at another's legs,
For which she made a wofull cry,
St. Swithun chanced for to come by,
Who made them all as sound, or more,
Than ever that they were before.

In Winchester Cathedral a statue depicting the old market-woman and her basket of eggs can still be seen.

Chroniclers also relate that Swithun used to travel to his pastoral appointments by night so as to avoid the pomp and ceremony that woul otherwise have accompanied him. Awareness that his son was more like Swithun than like Ealstan in disposition must have caused that tough old warrior Egbert some uneasy moments.

When in 823 (or 825) Ethelwulf, Ealstan and an alderman named Wulfherd, together with 'a large detachment from the main body of the army', were sent to Kent after the battle of Ellendune they met with quick success. *The Anglo-Saxon Chronicle* records that they 'drove Baldred, the king, northward over the Thames; whereupon the men of Kent immediately submitted to him (Ethelwulf), as did also the inhabitants of Surrey and Sussex and Essex'. Ethelwulf was appointed under-king of those four provinces, a post which he held till Egbert's death in 836, when he succeeded to the main kingdom of Wessex.

Returning then to Winchester, he installed his son Athelstan as under-king of Kent, Surrey, Sussex and Essex. Concerning this Athelstan, some mystery exists. According to Bishop Asser, who wrote a Life of Alfred the Great, Ethelwulf married his wife Osburga in 830, soon after he became under-king of Kent. Her sons are recorded as Ethelbald, Ethelbert, Ethelred and Alfred, and there was at least one daughter, Ethelswitha. Osburga is stated to have been the daughter of Oslac, who is variously described as steward, cup-bearer and butler to King Ethelwulf, but he is also said to have descended from the earliest Jutish invaders of the kingdom —a man of royal blood. Where, then, does Athelstan come in? The obvious inference is that Ethelwulf had been married before and that Athelstan was the child of this first marriage, unless he was illegitimate. But we do not know, and Athelstan fades out of the story. It is assumed that he died before his father, after ruling in Kent for an undetermined number of years.

Egbert died in 836. (That is the date given in *The Anglo-Saxon Chronicle*, though some modern scholars place it in 839, holding that all the *Chronicle* dates of this period are three years adrift. Without passing any opinion on the matter, for the sake of presenting a coherent story we stick to the dates given in *The Chronicle*. Those who prefer the current version of the chronology should add three years.) In the following year *The Chronicle* becomes obsessed with the Danes. They came in four successive years and evidently were almost everywhere victorious. The campaigns are recorded by *The Chronicle* as follows:

837. This year Alderman Wulfherd fought at Hamton with 33 pirates, and after great slaughter obtained the victory, but he died the same year. Alderman Ethelhelm also, with the men of Dorsetshire, fought with the Danish army in Portland-isle, and for a good while put them to flight; but in the end the Danes became masters of the field, and slew the alderman.

838. This year Alderman Herbert was slain by the heathens, and many men with him, among the Marshlanders. The same year, afterwards, in Lindsey, East Anglia and Kent, were many men slain by the army.

839. This year there was great slaughter in London, Canterbury and Rochester.

840. This year King Ethelwulf fought at Charmouth with thirty-five ships' crews, and the Danes remained masters of the place.

The picture we get is of sporadic raids in some force which are countered by local Saxon levies under the command of the local Alderman. 'Hamton' is Southampton; Alderman Wulfherd is the experienced warrior who had accompanied Ethelwulf to Kent 11 years previously. In the 840 raid Ethelwulf himself happened to be in that part of the kingdom and so led his troops into battle. He would be expected to be in the forefront of the fray, and there is no suggestion here, or at any other time, that he lacked courage. The front line of an Anglo-Saxon fyrd, facing Viking battle-axes, was no place for a coward.

After the encounter at Charmouth the realm was left in peace for five years. That was the result not so much of any trouncing the Saxons may have given the pirates as that in the year 840 Louis, the Holy Roman Emperor, died and the subsequent squabbling by his sons left the unhappy coasts of the Continent easier prey than the resolutely-defended kingdom of Wessex. The ruthless and notorious Viking, Ragnar Lodbrok, now appears upon the scene. In 845 he sent a fleet up the Seine to besiege

Paris. Twenty years later his fierce but gifted sons were to be the scourge of England.

In the same year, 845, the Danes were in Wessex again. This time they either rounded Land's End or launched their attack from Wales or Ireland, for the assault was made on the Somerset coast, where the river Parret offers a highway inland. Again they met their match. *The Anglo-Saxon Chronicle* records,

This year Alderman Eanwulf, with the men of Somersetshire, and Bishop Ealstan and Alderman Osric, with the men of Dorsetshire, fought at the mouth of the Parret with the Danish army; and there, after making a great slaughter, obtained the victory.

One senses in these victories of Ethelwulf's reign the influence of Egbert. He had clearly learned his lessons well in his participation in Charlemagne's wars. Not only were the West Saxons imbued with a fighting spirit but their organisation was good. Wherever the Danes struck they were met by an 'Alderman' with an efficient army. It is interesting, too, to see Bishop Ealstan again in the forefront of affairs. There followed six years of peace and then, in 851, the Danes renewed their onslaught with a pincer-movement, attacking at both ends of Wessex. First, they landed in Devon where they were brought to bay by 'Alderman Ceorl with the men of Devonshire' at a place which *The Chronicle* calls 'Wicgeanbeorg', identified by modern authorities as Wembury, a village near the mouth of the Yealm in the vicinity of Plymouth. The attack was in strength, for the records refer to 'the heathen *army*', (my italics, RW), but the Danes probably made a mistake in challenging the West Saxons at a point where they were doubtless strong and alert, on the borders of Devon and Cornwall where they had so recently had trouble with the Britons.

'The same year King Athelstan and Alderman Elchere fought in their ships and slew a large army at Sandwich in Kent, taking nine ships and dispersing the rest.' This is the first time we read of the English engaging in a sea-battle. Although Alfred is usually given the credit of founding the English navy, maybe the honour should go to Egbert. This, incidentally, is the last time that King Athelstan of Kent is mentioned. The probability is that he died soon afterwards.

The most dramatic event of the year, however, was the arrival of a fleet of Danish ships, stated by *The Anglo-Saxon Chronicle* to number 350, in the mouth of the Thames:

The crews went upon land and stormed Canterbury and London, putting to flight Beorhtwulf, king of the Mercians, with his army, and then marched southwards over the Thames into Surrey. Here Ethelwulf and his son

Ethelbald, at the head of the West Saxon army, fought with them at Aclea and made the greatest slaughter of the heathen army that we have ever heard reported of to this present day. There also they obtained the victory.

This was indeed a major battle. As was noted earlier, the Viking ships which have survived averaged 15 or 16 pairs of oars, so the crew of each would be not less than 30 men. One has to allow for a garrison left guarding the ships but, on the other hand, the army would doubtless pick up recruits on its way, so it looks as though the Danish forces would number about 10,000 men—if, that is, the number of ships was correctly recorded, which some modern authorities doubt. Again we see Ethelwulf, evidently not so mild on this occasion, leading his army. 'Aclea' is usually identified as Ockley, in Surrey.

In spite of all these defeats, the Danes were able to retire to Thanet where, for the first time, they wintered. The Kentish levies (under Alderman Eichere) and the men of Surrey (under Alderman Huda) attacked them there in 853 and 'soon obtained the victory; but there were many men slain and drowned on either hand, and both the aldermen killed'. In the following year the Danes, driven out of Thanet, still managed to winter in England, this time on the Isle of Sheppey. And now occur two almost incredible events which make one wonder just how seriously the menace of the Northmen was regarded. In the midst of all this fighting, while the Danes were still in Thanet,

Burhred, king of Mercia, besought King Ethelwulf to assist him to subdue North Wales. He did so; and with an army marched over Mercia into North Wales and made all the inhabitants subject to him.

It could be, of course, that the Danes or Norwegians were stirring up trouble in league with the Britons of North Wales, but the record sounds like a simple conquest. And again the allegedly unwarlike Ethelwulf was leading his army.

The other extraordinary development was that in 854, with the Danes wintering in Sheppey, Ethelwulf decided to make a pilgrimage to Rome. He travelled, says The Chronicle, 'with great pomp and was resident there a twelvemonth.' Either he had supreme faith in the military organization he left behind and the men in charge of it, or he was guilty of dangerous irresponsibility, or the Danes were regarded as little more than a nuisance. He was, of course, following a precedent, for other kings of Wessex had made the pilgrimage and two of them, Ina and Caedwalla, had died there. And perhaps he was able to make a better assessment of the situation than we can, for, in spite of being overseas for so long, he came back safely and found the kingdom intact.

In these pages we have quoted conflicting evidence concerning the character of Ethelwulf. He is described as sluggish, heavy, mild, devout, indolent, a disappointment to his vigorous father, unequal to the task of kingship; yet we also see him on several occasions leading his army into battle against ferocious enemies, maintaining the military organisation which his father had set up, and acting with commendable decision. Perhaps the explanation of the reputation he acquired lies in the extraordinary favour he showed to the Church. There were rumours extant that in his youth he had wanted to become a priest and had even taken holy orders. Now, when he was ordering affairs prior to embarking on the journey to Rome, he showed where his heart lay. As William of Malmesbury puts it, 'he granted every tenth hide of land within his kingdom to the servants of Christ, free from all tribute, exempt from all services'. William, who evidently had a copy of the charter in front of him as he wrote, quotes from the document,

Let it (the land in question) be free from all things, for the release of our souls, that it may be applied to God's service alone, exempt from expeditions, the building of bridges or of forts; in order that they may more diligently pour forth their prayers to God for us without ceasing.

It adds that 50 pslams had to be sung and two masses said at the churches of Winchester and Sherborne every Wednesday. When he arrived in Rome Ethelwulf made further splendid donations to the Church, which Asser lists as

a gold crown of four pounds in weight, two dishes of the purest gold, a sword richly set in gold, two gold images, silver-gilt Saxon urns, stoles bordered with gold and purple stripes, white silken garments for celebrating the mass, decorated with figures, and other costly articles of clothing. . . . He also bestowed rich alms in gold and silver on the bishops, the clergy and on the dwellers of Rome of every rank. . . . The Saxon schools, which had already been twice destroyed by fire since their establishment, he rebuilt at his own cost and further enriched them by the most liberal endowments.

He must have been a most welcome and popular guest in Rome.

In making such donations he again had a precedent, in the actions of no less a person than Charlemagne. Oppressed by forebodings about the future of his Empire and by his own approaching fate in the hereafter, Charlemagne had, in his last years, bequeathed three-quarters of the wealth in his treasury to his archbishops and bishops. But that he had his doubts about the efficacy of it all is illustrated by his comments on priests who 'buy land and serfs and other property and spend their time on banquets, oppression and robbery'. It may be that in Wessex Ethelwulf was better served by Swithun and Ealstan.

On his expedition to Rome Ethelwulf was accompanied by his youngest son, Alfred, who had already been there once, two years earlier, when, according to some probably biassed reports, he was anointed king by the Pope. Ethelwulf's overland journey to Rome lay through the domains of the Frankish king, Charles the Bald, with whom he was on excellent terms. Charles treated him with every honour and lent him a royal escort. On the return trek Ethelwulf spent many months at Charles' court, and his visit culminated in his marriage to Judith, Charles' daughter. It was a diplomatic marriage, for Ethelwulf was then a grey-haired man in his late fifties whereas Judith was thirteen. It is presumed that Osburga, Ethelwulf's previous wife and the mother of his sons, had died before he set out for Rome.

At the wedding ceremony, which took place at Charles' palace at Verberie, on the river Oise, occurred an incident which had unfortunate repercussions back in Wessex. Hincmar, the archbishop of Rheims, who performed the ceremony, placed a crown on Judith's head, thus ostensibly crowning her queen of Wessex. Now the West Saxons had a tradition, though it had existed for only three generations, that there should be no queen of Wessex. The king obviously had to have a wife, but she had no official position or political power. The taboo dated from the time of Beorhtric, who had been poisoned by his queen, Eadburga, daughter of Offa of Mercia. When the news of the coronation reached Wessex, therefore, Ethelwulf's nobles detected a sinister aspect in what had at first seemed the action of a foolish old man.

In his absence Wessex had been governed and administered quite efficiently by his council of ministers, among whom the chiefs were Swithun, Ealstan and Ethelwulf's eldest surviving son, Ethelbald. Now that Ethelwulf was on the point of returning, there was a division among them. *The Chronicle* intimates that the people were glad to see him, but evidently many of those in authority preferred the tough and energetic Ethelbald as their leader. The incident of the crowning of Judith seems to have tipped the scales against Ethelwulf. Civil war threatened but Ethelwulf, that man of peace, averted the danger by stepping down. He agreed that Ethelbald should take over the kingdom of Wessex and that he himself should retire to Kent, with Sussex, Surrey and Essex as satellites— the kingdom, in fact, over which he ruled in the time of his father Egbert. At his age he placed little value on the exercise of power, as long as he had sufficient means to maintain his accustomed standard of living. He went away quite happily to Kent, where he was well received and where Judith was allowed to sit on a throne by his side.

He died about two years later, apparently in 858. His was not an unsuccessful reign. He had lost nothing of the enlarged realm left to him by his father. Danish inroads had been repulsed and, for a time, the land was at peace. By the other kingdoms of Britain he was acknowledged as a leader, though he made no attempt to enforce supremacy. To what extent this was all due to his talented council and what to Ethelwulf himself remains unknown. Perhaps the facts that he was able to recognise good advice and humble enough to take it mark him as an exceptional man in that headstrong age.

VI

The Sons of Ethelwulf
and the Fall of the North

The reign of Ethelbald in Wessex began between two and three years before his father's death in 858. It seems that there was tacit agreement that the King of Wessex had a kind of overlordship over Kent, Surrey, Sussex and Kent, to which Ethelwulf had retired. The rest of Ethelwulf's family, including his sons Ethelbert, Ethelred and Alfred, evidently accompanied their father to Kent and, on Ethelwulf's death, no objection was made to Ethelbert succeeding him there.

The family seems to have been an unusually harmonious one, though with Ethelbald perhaps the odd man out. As we have seen, their father Ethelwulf was a mild, unambitious man, while their mother, Osburga, seems to have been an exceptional woman. The dispute which split the kingdom on Ethelwulf's return from Rome was evidently due to an honest determination on the part of one faction in the Council to safeguard the realm against the external dangers which they could see developing, rather than to the ambition of Ethelbald, though undoubtedly they saw in Ethelbald a bold, forceful young man who could be trusted to act energetically. It is significant that Ealstan, the militant Bishop of Sherborne, and a senior Alderman, Eanwulf of Somerset, sided with Ethelbald. Anyway, wise counsels in which Swithun must have played a leading part averted the civil war which, under other circumstances, might easily have resulted.

Ethelbald has been poorly treated by history, largely because most of the chroniclers who mention him at all have been monks, and he committed a heinous crime in the eyes of the Church—he married his father's widow, Judith, who was still only in her 'teens. William of Malmesbury calls him 'base and perfidious'; Asser says he was headstrong and arbitrary. Ethelbald must also have offended many of the West Saxon aristocrats by marrying a crowned queen. But we get the impression that Ethelbald cared nothing for all that. Another adjective which Asser uses of him is 'audacious', and it may well be that the West Saxon Council were prepared to shut their eyes to a lot of faults in return for a vigorous king. His early death in 860 seems to have been widely mourned, and there are no records of the Danes giving any trouble while Ethelbald was alive.

After his death the succession was provided for by Ethelwulf's will. He had decreed that on his own death Ethelbert should succeed him on the throne of Kent. If Ethelbald were to die childless (which is what happened), Ethelbert would continue to reign in Kent while Ethelred, the next son, would take over in Wessex. To this, the Witan, or General Council of the realm, had agreed. However, we find Ethelbert becoming king of the united kingdom of Wessex, Kent, Essex, Surrey and Sussex. As there is no record of any discord, and as the other brothers continued to work together, it must be assumed that they agreed. As already stated, they were an unusual family.

Little is known of Ethelbert, who lived for only another five years. And nothing is recorded as to the causes of the deaths of these young kings. We can arrive at some sort of inference about their ages. We know that Alfred was born at Wantage soon after Christmas, 849. His sister, Ethelswitha, was about 14 years older, which would put her birth in 835 and make her fourteen when she married King Burhred of Mercia in 853. Although there was thus a considerable gap between the two younger children of the family, it seems likely that there was about two years between each of the others. Ethelbald accompanied his father to the Witan of the year 850 and also to the war which culminated in the battle of Aclea in 851, which implies that by then he had come of age. If that means he was twenty-one in 850, then he would have been born in 829, Ethelbert in 831, and Ethelred in 833, which fits in exactly with Ethelswitha's birth in 835.

At the time of his death in 860, therefore, Ethelbald would have been thirty-one. Ethelbert would have been thirty-five when he died in 866, and Ethelred's age at the time of his death in 871 would have been thirty-eight. Ethelred is said by some chroniclers to have died worn out by the rigours of the campaign against the Danes but by others to have perished from his wounds. That did certainly not apply to Ethelbald or Ethelbert. At some point along the line an hereditary weakness seems to have been introduced into the royal family of Wessex. Alfred himself suffered greatly from a mysterious malady, and the good work accomplished by a number of the later monarchs of the dynasty was frustrated by their early deaths.

In Ethelbert's short reign the attacks by the Danes were resumed. A section of the heathen army which had been plundering on the Continent crossed the Channel and in a surprise assault stormed Winchester, the chief city of Wessex. Again the military organsiation initiated by Egbert proved its worth. Although too late to prevent the raid, the men of Hampshire and Berkshire, under Alderman Osric and Alderman Ethelwulf cut off the intruders before they could regain their ships and defeated them in a bloody battle, recovering 'immense booty'. The Danes, said Asser, 'fled like so many women'.

The survivors, however, made their way around the coast to Thanet, where they encamped and were joined by others from Europe. In the year 865 they signed a treaty with the men of Kent, whereby the latter thought they had secured peace in return for the payment of a large sum of money. But

these robbers knew nothing of truth and good faith; they were well aware that they should obtain a much larger sum by pillage than by treaties of peace. Scarcely was the league concluded than they again broke it and like cunning foxes secretly and by night left their camp and ravaged all the eastern side of Kent.

Such was the contemporary view of the Danes. The English chroniclers are bitter about their perfidy: they complain that time and again the Danes swore the most sacred oaths, on talismans of their own choosing, and straightway broke them. But what the English failed to understand was that they were continually dealing with different leaders. A Danish commander, cornered and forced to conclude a treaty, would usually though not always keep his word, but as he retired to look for his fortune elsewhere his place would be taken by a new horde, and often many of his followers would switch to the new leader.

865 was a fateful year for England. Twenty years earlier the notorious Viking Ragnar Lodbrok ('Hairy Breeches') had, after attacking Paris and losing many men through an epidemic of plague, turned his attention to Northumbria. There, according to tradition, he was captured and thrown to die in 'the Serpent Tower of Ella', the Northumbrian king. His deathsong, as he lay in this pit of adders (or, according to some versions, of conger eels), became a favourite with the Viking skalds, or minstrels.

Sir Winston Churchill, in his *History of the English-speaking Peoples*, quotes the version, in Norse poetry, of how Ragnar's sons heard the news of how their father died:

Bjorn 'Ironside' gripped his spear shaft so hard that the print of his fingers remained stamped upon it. Hvitserk was playing chess, but he clenched his fingers upon a pawn so tightly that the blood started from under his nails. Sigurd 'Snake-eye' was trimming his nails with a knife, and kept on paring until he cut into the bone. Ivar 'the Boneless' demanded the precise details of his father's execution and his face 'became red, blue and pale by turns, and his skin was swollen with anger'.

This Ivar was a military strategist of the first order. For years he directed the Danish fleets on their marauding expeditions, striking first here and then there, and moving his forces like the carved men on a chessboard. Now he determined that the time had come for vengeance on Northumbria, and linked with that was an ambitious plan for the conquest and subjugation of all England.

The incursion of the Danes into Kent was only a part of a vast campaign. From Denmark and from the coasts of Europe where they had been plundering, ships beyond number converged on East Anglia. There, says *The Chronicle*, 'they fixed their winter quarters, where they were soon horsed; and the inhabitants made peace with them'. (Incidentally, this entry in *The Anglo-Saxon Chronicle* is for the year 866, but it has been established that as *The Chronicle* was using a calendar which began in September, the year in question is really 865.) The invading army spent, in fact, the best part of a year in East Anglia, preparing for their stroke. Then, in the autumn of 866, they moved inland and marched to York.

The Danes were past-masters at intrigue and diplomacy as well as of war, and they well knew how to take advantage of opportunities. The Northumbrians were less farsighted. Ignoring the menace on their doorstep, they had become involved in a civil war between the forces of their king Osbert, who had reigned for 18 years, and one Aella, who was trying to depose him. While they were thus squabbling, they found that the Danes had moved suddenly and occupied York. Probably it was a combined land-and-sea operation. It is clear, from this and subsequent campaigns, that the Danes had mastered the secret of the system of Roman roads, which were still the main highways of Britain. Alarmed at last, the warring rivals in Northumbria managed to patch up their quarrel, an exercise which took four months, and prepared to attack the city. The Danes moved into York on 1 November; the first assault was made on them on 21 March of the following year (867). The Northumbrian army is described as a 'vast force', and it met with some success, breaking into York at several points. In the ferocious battle, however, both of the rival kings were killed, as well as great numbers of the Northumbrians. The Danes remained in possession of York and were later in the year able to instal a puppet king, named Egbert, to govern Northumbria. With this preliminary settled, they moved over to Nottingham, which was within the kingdom of Mercia.

The Mercian king Burhred, had, as we have noted, married Ethelswitha, King Ethelwulf's daughter, and was therefore closely allied with the royal family of Wessex. The bonds had been further cemented in 868 by the marriage of Alfred with Elswitha, the daughter of Ethelred Mucel, Earl of the Gaini (who lived in the vicinity of Gainsborough), who was related to the Mercian royal family. The Mercians therefore had no hesitation about sending an urgent plea for help to the West Saxons. The new king of Wessex, Ethelred, who had recently succeeded Ethelbert, immediately responded. His army arrived at Nottingham and attacked the Danes, who were busily fortifying the place. 'But,' says *The Chronicle* with veiled disgust, 'there was no heavy fight; for the Mercians made peace with the army.'

The West Saxon army returned to Wessex, and the Danes, after a time, retired to York. There they remained for a year, gathering their strength, while the English kingdoms did the same, with varying success.

The first kingdoms to be put to the test were East Anglia and Mercia. In the autumn of 869 a part of the Danish army moved south, evidently mostly by road, and crossing Mercia without hindrance, settled down to winter quarters in Thetford. About the same time, another contingent of Danes landed in Lincolnshire and sacked the monastery of Bardney. Hearing of this the local Alderman, Algar, collected his forces and went to intercept the raiders. On 21 September he met the Danes somewhere in Kesteven and at first defeated them. During the night, however, another Danish army arrived on the scene and joined their comrades. In the morning the battle was resumed and continued throughout the entire day. Towards sunset the Danes staged a retreat, thus tempting the Angles to break rank and pursue them. They then turned, re-formed and slaughtered the disordered Angles. The survivors, led by Algar, made an heroic stand on a hill, but eventually all lay dead. Only a handful of boys escaped.

Very shortly afterwards the Danes arrived at the abbey of Croyland, which they sacked and pillaged. From there they went on to Medhamstede (Peterborough), 'burning and breaking and slaying abbot and monks and all that they there found. They made such havoc there that a monastery, which was before full rich, was now reduced to nothing.' The horde then passed on to Huntingdon and Ely, which were also destroyed. The words by which a chronicler of the same century described the scene in northern France, after the passage of the Danes, now applied to England:

There did not exist a road which was not littered with dead, including priests, women and children. Despair spread through the land, and it seemed that all Christian people would perish.

Meantime the Danes at Thetford were attacked by the local Alderman Ulfketel, who was killed in the battle. The East Anglian king, Edmund, then took up the conflict. The armies met in a battle in the neighbourhood of Hoxne, which resulted in a complete victory for the Danes. According to a strong tradition, Edmund was captured and shot to death with arrows—a fate which earned him prompt canonisation, for he seems to have been revered as a saint and martyr within 25 or 30 years of his death. The Danes in East Anglia are said to have been under the command of Hingwar and Hubba—Hingwar being the same person as Ivar the Boneless. Another character who first appears in the annals at this time is Guthrum, who soon afterwards was Alfred's chief antagonist. He was one of the leaders who arrived overnight to reinforce the army which defeated Algar.

With East Anglia entirely crushed and Mercia paralysed, the Danish army now moved into Wessex. No doubt they had rightly judged that that was where the main opposition would lie. Once they had overcome the West Saxon army, which they had seen in action at Nottingham as well as in their raids on the Wessex coast, they had little to fear from any other quarter. Some of them therefore marched overland and others made their way by ship up the Thames, plundering on all sides, and arrived at a rendezvous at Reading. Here, on a peninsula at the confluence of the Thames and the Kennet, the West Saxon kings had a palace or fortress, which the Danes occupied. About half of them stayed at Reading, improving the fortifications of the place by building a wall, or earthwork, across the peninsula, while the other half went out foraging.

This second band was met by the local Alderman, Ethelwulf, at a place called Englafield, which was probably Englefield. In a desperate fight one of the Danish earls was killed, with many of his men. The rest fled. Four days later King Ethelred, with Alfred as his second-in-command, arrived on the scene with an army they had been collecting. They shut the Danes up within their fortress at Reading and began a siege, killing anyone who ventured outside the gates. But the Danes, taking advantage of a moment when the West Saxons were engaged in pitching camp, made a sudden sally. A hard-fought battle ensued, in which first one side and then the other seemed to be winning, but eventually the Danes got the better of it and chased the English off the field. Ethelwulf, the brave alderman, was killed and according to Asser, the Danes afterwards dragged his body as far as Derby. Ethelred and Alfred escaped by crossing the Thames near Windsor, 'by a ford which was unknown to the Danes'.

Another four days elapsed and then, having collected their scattered troops, the West Saxon brothers tried again. This time the two armies met on the chalk downland ridge overlooking the Vale of the White Horse, at a place which *The Chronicle* calls Aescesdune and which was probably Ashdown, or Aston. Here occurred a major battle, and the records have preserved considerable details about it and about the disposition of the armies. The Danes had taken command of the hill-crest and had concealed themselves in low, thick scrub, from which they aimed showers of arrows at the Saxons down below. Their army was divided into two sections, one commanded by two kings, Bagseg and Halfdan, and the other by a group of earls. Apparently in accordance with the rules of precedence, Ethelred lined up his troops to face the kings, while Alfred, being of lower rank, took on the earls.

At least that was the idea, but Ethelred, a devout man, lingered overlong in his tent at the foot of the hill, hearing mass. The Saxon army waited impatiently, harassed all the time by arrows, but still the king did not appear. At last Alfred could bear it no longer. Giving the signal to attack he rushed up the hill, say the chroniclers, like a wild boar, and the troops were glad to follow him. Closing with the enemy, they engaged in a fierce hand-to-hand struggle which lasted all through the day. Soon Ethelred had joined in, and some modern commentators have suggested that the appearance of his fresh troops, when the Danes were thinking that all of their enemies were already engaged, may have been the deciding factor. Be that as it may, the English won. Ethelred himself is said to have slain king Bagseg, and five Danish earls were among the killed. The Danes were pursued throughout the night back to Reading, and all stragglers were massacred. The West Saxons were exultant. But the Danes stayed in Reading, and only a fortnight later were ready to fight again.

This time the battle-field was at Basing, and the Danes had the advantage, though a Saxon chronicler, making the best of it, says 'they carried off no spoils'. Then reinforcements arrived at Reading for the heathen army, and the West Saxons evidently retired. No doubt frequent skirmishes occurred, and no doubt the Danes raided and plundered wherever they could, but most of the details of the war are lost. About two months after the fight at Basing we find Ethelred and Alfred engaged in a pitched battle at a place called, in *The Anglo-Saxon Chronicle*, Meredune. Numerous unsatisfactory attempts to identify this place have been made—a possible locality is Marden, near Devizes, in which case the Danes would have penetrated to the heart of Wessex. *The Chronicle* says that, as at Ashdown, the Danes were in two divisions and that Ethelred and Alfred

put them to flight, enjoying the victory for some time during the day; and there was much slaughter on either hand; but the Danes became masters of the field.

One theory suggests that the West Saxons had been driven even farther into their homeland and that the battle took place at Martin, in Hampshire. Its protagonists point out that soon afterwards King Ethelred died at Wimborne, or, according to one tradition, at Witchampton, near Wimborne, and one chronicler (John of Brompton) says that he died in agony, caused by his wounds. This would suggest a battle in the vicinity, which would fit Martin. We cannot know, but the imagination is fired by the thought of these heroic encounters occurring in the familiar surroundings of the quiet English countryside. We can visualise the Roman roads and the now overgrown Saxon 'harrow-ways' clattering to the tramp of armed men. Red-haired Danes with blood dripping from their battle-axes charge with wild war-cries out of the mist. Corpses hang from the convenient limbs of oak-trees; kites and ravens, now long extinct in many English counties, scream and croak over the battle-fields; the frightened eyes of women and children peer from the thorny refuge of blackthorn thickets; straying cattle, their owners dead, vanish into the forest. But every village, every stream, bears a familiar name. The stormclouds of smoke, the tongues of flame, are from the burning thatch of huts, not from stubble-fields, but, even so, this was England.

Ethelred, like his brothers before him, reigned for only a few years—five, in fact. We have little information about his character. He is reported to have been mild and affable, and his behaviour before the battle of Ashdown shows that he was almost excessively devout. That he was peaceable is indicated by the way in which he agreed with his brothers when a more aggressive person would have disputed the succession. Yet he was a redoubtable warrior when he had to be as is demonstrated by his valour at Ashdown, when with his own hand he killed the Danish king. Perhaps we can set him down as a junior version of his father Ethelwulf. It is no mean commendation.

VII

The Campaigns of Alfred

A sword age, a wind age, a wolf age,
No longer is there mercy among men.

So ran a Norse skald's vision of the end of the world, and for the English of the 870s it must have seemed that Doomsday had arrived. The death of Ethelred imposed no break in the catalogue of horrors, no hiatus in the offensive by the Danes. Even while Alfred was attending his brother's funeral they were engaged in battle at Reading. It seems that the Danish garrison there received reinforcements—'a vast army' (says *The Chronicle*) of Vikings come over for the summer plundering. These set about and thoroughly defeated a small English force that had been keeping watch on the fortified camp.

Ethelred died soon after Easter. He left two infant sons who, in happier times, might have succeeded to at least part of the kingdom, though there was no certainty about it. The West Saxon Witan could choose whichever member of the royal family seemed to fit the role best, and in this instance there was no doubt at all about their choice. Alfred took over automatically, though with a minimum of ceremony; we read no accounts of coronation celebrations. Within a month he was engaged in another major battle with the Danes, and was again defeated.

This affair took place at Wilton, in Wiltshire. The wording of the record in *The Anglo-Saxon Chronicle* seems to imply that the English were once again caught by a typical Danish ruse. The Danes pretended to run away and then, when their pursuers were scattered, turned round and massacred them. Alfred was learning his lessons the hard way. Summing up that dreadful year, 871, *The Chronicle* states:

This year were nine general battles fought with the Army in the kingdom south of the Thames; besides those skirmishes, in which Alfred the king's brother, and every single alderman, and the thanes of the king, oft rode against them; which were accounted nothing. This year also were slain nine earls and one king. . . .

To this last achievement the English clung for comfort. And they long remembered their first great victory, the battle of Ashdown. It was really their only success of the year, and though it did not amount to much militarily, it did wonders for their morale: they had met the dreaded heathen face to face and had beaten them. They had chased the flying enemy across the Vale, killing them by hundreds as they scampered towards the safety of their camp. It showed that the thing could be done. Meantime, Alfred viewed the situation pragmatically. As Sir Winston Churchill put its, 'he thought it best to come to terms while he still had an army.' *The Chronicle* records that he made peace with the Danes, a settlement which doubtless involved handing over to them a huge payment. They seem to have stayed in Wessex till they had collected their booty, then, in 872, they sailed downstream from Reading and took over London, where they made their winter quarters.

The phrase 'made peace with the Army' now runs like a refrain through *The Chronicle* entries, year after year. In 871 it was the West Saxons who 'made peace with the Army'. In 872, with the Danes on Mercian territory in London, it was the Mercians. In 873 is the significant entry, 'The Mercians again made peace with the Army'. The Danes, having disposed of all the tribute from the previous year, came back for more. A surviving document of this year records the sale of land belonging to the Bishop of Worcester in order to raise money to pay the Danes in London.

The peace that Alfred purchased—and he must have paid a very high price for it—lasted five years. The only warlike action recorded for Wessex in that period was in 875 when, in the language of *The Anglo-Saxon Chronicle*, 'this summer King Alfred went out to sea with an armed fleet and fought with seven ship-rovers, one of whom he took and dispersed the others'. We can assume that Alfred was using the respite well. As well as training and reorganising his army he now had an 'armed fleet' capable of meeting the Vikings in their own element.

During those five years the Danes were preoccupied in the Midlands and North. First, in 872, there was trouble in Northumbria, the Northumbrians staging a revolt against Egbert, the puppet king whom they had set up. They sent a detachment of the army up to deal with this insubordination but apparently failed to do so, for a new king of Northumbrian choice, named Ricsige, managed to reign for three years and then died a natural death. Probably Northumbria had been so devastated in previous years that the meagre pickings that remained seemed hardly worth fighting for. The entire Danish army spent the winter at Torksey, in Lincolnshire.

In the spring they moved over into Mercia, whose long history of independence now ceased. In a war the details of which are unrecorded, the Mercians were beaten. King Burhred, after reigning for 22 years, escaped to the Continent, where he made his way to Rome. He died there and was buried in the Saxon school which Ethelwulf had endowed. In Mercia the Danes set up another puppet, a man named Ceolwulf whom *The Chronicle* categorizes as 'unwise', on humiliating terms. Says *The Chronicle*,

He swore oaths to them and gave hostages, that it should be ready for them on whatever day they would have it; and he would be ready with himself and with all those that would remain with him, at the service of the Army.

The Army spent the winter at Repton, a former royal town in the middle of Mercia. In 875 it split. One contingent, under a leader named Halfdan, went north and camped by the river Tyne. From there marauding parties roamed far and wide through Northumbria and the neighbouring states of Pictland and Strathclyde. Provided there was plunder to be had it mattered not at all to the Vikings what nationality were the people whom they were robbing. Meantime the other and larger section of the Danish Army moved over to Cambridge, where they camped for a year.

But now the scene was changing. The old leaders of the Danes were dying, mostly in the incessant wars, and new ones were coming to the front. Halfdan apparently left some of his followers in Northumbria while he himself went off raiding in northern Ireland, where he is thought to have been killed in battle in 877. Ivar the Boneless died, apparently at peace, in Dublin in 872. The army at Cambridge was under the leadership of Guthrum, Oscytel and Anund.

More important, there were at last signs that these restless sea-rovers were willing to settle down. At least, some of them were. One can appreciate that middle-aged Vikings, with the booty they had collected in years of raiding, would become aware of the advantages of a sedentary life. They wanted halls and fields and servants of their own, with their families growing up around them, and that was impossible back in Denmark and Norway whence overcrowding had driven them in the first place. But here, in the West, were lands more fertile than their homeland, which they could have for the taking. Many of them had doubtless taken (by force or otherwise) English wives. And for many of them slaves were part of the booty they had acquired on their expeditions. For the year 876 *The Anglo-Saxon Chronicle* records, 'Halfdan divided the land of the Northumbrians; so that they became afterwards their harrowers and ploughers'.

The Danes, in fact, took the southern part of the kingdom, comprising approximately Yorkshire and Lancashire, under their direct rule and left the northern section under the control of English kings, though probably with a good deal of Danish supervision. Evidently the local population in the Danish half was reduced, in general, to the level of serfs. Much the same was happening in Frankland where later (in 911) the Viking leader, Rollo, took possession of Normandy and founded there the kingdom which in due course was to produce William the Conqueror.

It was this desire to settle down that may well account for the comparative success of the peace treaty which Alfred imposed on Guthrum after the battle of Ethandune. We can imagine that over at Cambridge Guthrum and his associates were confronted with divided counsels. The younger men, who still had their fortunes to make, wanted more raids, more pillaging, more looting; the older ones were more inclined to be content with what they had. As it happened, the first party had the initial advantage. The demands to launch yet another attack on defiant Wessex and so acquire the wealth of that still largely intact kingdom doubtless coincided with the natural inclinations of these Danish pirate-kings. But when, eventually, the campaign ended in ignominious defeat, the peace party gained the ascendancy.

The first sign of the new war occurred in 876, when 'the Army stole into Wareham, a fort of the West Saxons'. It can be regarded as a diversionary move designed to weaken the Wessex defences elsewhere, for, with the main Danish camp at Cambridge and the Thames as roughly the land frontier, Wareham is about the last place where an attack would be expected. However, Alfred was alert and soon had the place surrounded; the Danes found they had walked into a trap. It did not suit them at all to be shut up in a fortress with their backs to the sea, when what they had wanted was a few weeks or months let loose over an unpillaged countryside, so they offered to parley. If Alfred would let them out, they said, they would leave this kingdom, and they swore to do so on their 'holy bracelet smeared with the blood of sacrificial animals' which, says The Chronicle, they had never before done with any other nation. But no sooner had the terms been settled and Alfred's guard relaxed than 'their horsemen stole by night into Exeter'.

Evidently the Danish forces in Wareham were very considerable, for even after all those who had horses had escaped and galloped across country to Exeter there were still plenty left within the fortifications. These now prepared to leave by sea. 'They sailed west about,' says The Chronicle, 'until they met with a great mist at sea, and there perished one hundred and twenty ships at Swanage'. Holiday-makers at Swanage can still see along the south side of the bay the half-submerged reef on which the Danish fleet, lost in the mist, foundered. The number of Danish casualties was probably at least 4000.

Meantime Alfred with a force of cavalry had followed hard on the heels of the Danes to Exeter but had failed to catch up with them before they gained the safety of the fortress there. So again Alfred, unable to smoke them out, had to parley. 'They gave him as many hostages as he required,' states *The Chronicle*, 'swearing with solemn oaths to observe the strictest amity.' Escorted by Alfred's troops, they rode, doubtless along the Fosse Way, out of Wessex and arrived in Mercia about harvest-time. 'Some of the harvest they divided among themselves, and some they gave to Ceolwulf'. Those were hard times for the Mercian peasants.

Winter descended on the tormented land, and the campaigning season came to an end. Or that is what usually happened, and Alfred and his court, relaxing for a short time from their exertions, kept Christmas at Chippenham. But just after Twelfth Night, the feast of the Epiphany, the Danish army, ignoring all precedent, appeared outside the royal town. Alfred and his family just managed to escape; his courtiers and thanes were scattered and the Danes, entering Chippenham, made it their winter quarters and proceeded to plunder the countryside far and wide. Many of Alfred's supporters fled overseas to Frankland. 'The people who remained,' says Asser,

were reduced to the condition of servants and beggars by their cruel oppressors, and both country and people were in the wildest disorder.

The triumph of the Danes seemed complete. Only Alfred remained and he, says *The Chronicle*, 'with a little band uneasily sought the woods and fastnesses of the moors.' The Danes had evidently been right in their belief that Wessex could be conquered, in spite of the formidable resistance it had put up so far.

The events that occurred between Twelfth Night and Whitsuntide of the year 878 are so crucial in English history that they deserve attention in some detail. Writers in subsequent ages have rightly regarded Alfred as the prototype of the Englishman who refuses to accept that he is beaten, and they have been right, too, in asserting that his spring campaign alone saved England from complete Danish domination. But, properly understood, the course of the war in that year reveals Alfred as a master strategist—a military commander of genius. Unfortunately, this last aspect of his character has been obscured by faulty reconstruction of the campaign, based on mistaken identification of the place-names mentioned.

Let us read again what *The Anglo-Saxon Chronicle*, our main informant concerning the events of 878, has to say:

In the Easter of this year King Alfred with his little force raised a work at Athelney; from which he assailed the Army, assisted by that part of Somersetshire which was nearest to it. Then, in the seventh week after Easter, he rode to Ecgbryhtes-stane by the eastern side of Selwood; and there came to meet him all the people of Somersetshire and Wiltshire and that part of Hampshire which is on this side of the sea, and they rejoiced to see him. Then within one night he went from this retreat to Acglea; and within one night after he proceeded to Ethandune; and there fought with all the Army, and put them to flight, riding after them as far as the fortress, where he remained a fortnight. Then the Army gave him hostages with many oaths, that they would go out of his kingdom. They told him also that their king would receive baptism. And they did accordingly; for in the course of three weeks after, King Guthrum, attended by some thirty of the worthiest men that were in the Army, came to him at Aller, which is near Athelney, and there the king became his sponsor in baptism; and his crisom-loosing was at Wedmore. He was there twelve nights with the king, who honoured him and his attendants with many presents.

Such are the bald facts of the story. Asser, King Alfred's biographer, adds a number of details. Of Alfred as a refugee in Somerset he writes,

And at that time King Alfred, with a few of his nobles and some warriors and vassals besides, led an unquiet life in great tribulation in the woodland and marshy parts of Somerset. For he had nothing on which to live except what he could win by frequent sallies, either openly or by stealth, from the pagans or from the Christians who had submitted to the pagans' rule.

Of the meeting of Alfred with his troops at Ecgbryhthes-stane he says,

And when the king was seen, receiving him as was right as one returned from the dead after such tribulation, they were filled with boundless joy.

And of the battle of Ethandune,

he fought against all the Army in a dense, shield-locked array, and, long maintaining a stubborn fight, and length by the Divine will he obtained the victory and overthrow the pagans with the greatest slaughter, and, striking down the fugitives, followed them as far as their stronghold. And all that he found outside the stronghold he seized, whether men, horses or cattle, slaying the men at once. And before the gates of the pagan stronghold he with all his army manfully pitched his camp. And when he had tarried there for fourteen days, the pagans, worn out with hunger, fear and cold, at last in despair sought peace on this condition, that the King should receive from them as many hostages as he chose to name, while he himself should give them none, these being such terms of peace as they had never before concluded with anyone. . . .

To the campaign there was also a preliminary encounter which is usually regarded as a separate incident but which has to be viewed as an integral and important development of the war. *The Anglo-Saxon Chronicle*, again for the year 878, describes it as follows:

In the winter of the same year the brother of Ingwar (Ivar the Boneless) and Halfdan landed in Wessex, in Devonshire, with three and twenty ships; and there was he slain, and eight hundred men with him, and forty of his army. There was also taken the war flag, which they called the Raven.

Again Asser contributes additional information. He says that the Danish captain (who is by other chroniclers identified as Ubba) 'sailed from the region of Demetia (Pembrokeshire) and where he had wintered after many slaughters of the Christians made there'. The place of his landing is *Cynuit*, a stronghold before which he came to 'a wretched ending while acting rashly' . . .

For in that stronghold many of the king's servants had shut themselves with their men for safety. But when the pagans saw that the stronghold was unprepared and altogether unfortified, except only that it had walls constructed in our fashion, they would not assault it, because the place is by the nature of the ground very secure on every side except the east, but began to besiege it, thinking that those men within would soon be compelled to surrender by hunger and thirst and by the blockade, since there is no water adjoining that stronghold. But it did not turn out as they thought. For the Christians, before they at all submitted to suffer such misery, inspired by heaven and thinking it far better to earn either death or victory, unexpectedly sally out on the pagans at dawn, and from the first onset overthrow the enemy, slaying them, together with their king, for the most part, though a few fled and escaped to their ships.

The sequence of the events, both in *The Chronicle* and in Asser, is first the surprise attack on Chippenham and Alfred's flight to the marshes of Somerset; then Ubba's attack by sea; and finally Alfred's campaign culminating in the battle of Ethandune.

Now, the conventional notion is that the fortress to which Alfred chased the Danes after the battle of Ethandune was Chippenham. Once this is accepted, the natural thing is to look for the battle site somewhere on the downs between Ecgbryhthes-stane (usually identified as a point near Brixton Deverill, in west Wiltshire) and Chippenham. And one offers itself—Edington, a pleasant little village under the downland scarp that is the northern limit of Salisbury Plain. The theory (quite erroneous) that Westbury White Horse was carved on a neighbouring hillside to commemorate the battle is sometimes quoted as additional evidence.

There is, however, an alternative site in Somerset which makes much better sense of the whole story. As one who is familiar with both sites and has studied each of them on the spot, the present writer has no hesitation in accepting the Somerset one—though, as a Wiltshireman, he would be naturally biassed in favour of the Wiltshire site if the evidence were not overwhelmingly against it. The following reconstruction summarises what probably happened and incidentally reveals Alfred as the military genius he undoubtedly was. When Alfred and his small party fled from Chippenham in mid-January he rode through the dense Forest of Selwood—for centuries a natural boundary between Wiltshire and Somerset—crossed the Fosse Way and took refuge in the Somerset marshland. At that time lowland Somerset was an oozy, amphibious region, especially in winter—a country of bogs, creeks, willows, will-o'-the-wisps, mud-flats, reed-beds and meandering rivers. It was possible for ships to venture as far inland as Glastonbury and Ilchester. The isle of Athelney was virtually inaccessible to anyone unfamiliar with the secret marshland ways.

But the Danes knew where he was. It is not to be supposed that they let him escape and then sat down carelessly at Chippenham to feast. On the contrary, they were exceedingly active, plundering far and wide, and they were also keeping an eye on Alfred. That was easy enough, for from a number of hills, which were then headlands overlooking a watery morass, it was possible to watch Athelney. The most obvious place is the ridge of the Polden Hills, a narrow but steep hog's-back of a hill which runs westwards as a finger-like peninsula, almost to Bridgwater. Within a few miles of its base runs the Fosse Way. We may be sure that the Danes sent a sizeable contingent of their army down the old Roman road and out onto the Poldens, and probably to some of the other hills which offered vantage-points. We remember *The Chronicle* says that after Alfred had fortified Athelney, 'from that work he waged war untiringly against the Army'. That implies that they were somewhere in the vicinity, and not 60 or 70 miles away at Chippenham.

As the winter wore on, Guthrum, seeing that he was having no success in his skirmishes with Alfred, called up a Danish fleet. One was at hand in Demetia, under the leadership of Ubba, a son of the renowned Ragnar Lodbrok. All it had to do was to cross the Bristol Channel and creep up the flooded river Parret. Its ships could anchor almost under the walls of Athelney. Ubba sailed upstream as far as the first ford, where an old road from the Midlands to north Devon crossed the river. This ford was defended by a small fort known as Combwich (as the village still is), which in some medieval documents is written as Cyneth. Here is probably the 'Cynuit' at which occurred the dramatic battle in which Ubba was killed. The capture of the Raven banner, incidentally, must have given a marvellous boost to Saxon morale and have been correspondingly depressing to the Danes. It had been reputedly woven in a single day by the three daughters of Ragnar Lodbrok and went before the Vikings into battle. When it waved exuberantly, that was a sign of victory; when it hung limp, of defeat.

The defeat of the fleet and the death of Ubba, coupled with the omen of the capture of the Raven banner, must have been throughly depressing to Guthrum. However, he persevered with his blockade of Athelney and, says a later chronicler,

summoned from all parts the men who had settled in England and had occupied fortresses in the hills, ordering them to quit these and join the army. He saw that there was danger in delay. . . .

Much of this great army assembled on the Poldens, watching Athelney and probably waiting for the marshes to dry up sufficiently with the onset of summer for an assault to be feasible. Leaving behind most of his soldiers to keep the enemy occupied, Alfred and a few followers slipped out one night and made their way eastwards to Selwood. It is possible to do this on horse-back, following lanes that were probably roads in Saxon days, without being visible to watchers on the Poldens. The present writer has done so.

An army would be able to assemble in force in the shelter of Selwood without being seen by the enemy. Alfred now proceeded to execute one of those swift marches across country which the Danes had employed to his discomfiture on more than one occasion, as at Wareham, Exeter and, finally, Chippenham. On the second day he was on the ridge of the Poldens, and the Danes were trapped.

The ridge is in places less than half-a-mile wide and bounded on either side by what were then completely impassable fens—there was no escape. Hence Asser's insistence on the shield-wall; the Danes had to break through that before even one of them could hope for safety.

And there, in the narrowest part of the peninsula, is a village named Edington.

The Danes, knowing their situation, must have been at a psychological disadvantage. They fought well, as usual, but with a sense of doom. At last they broke and fled, and there was only one way they could go. They ran to the end of the hills, where they dip down to the Parret, and there took refuge in a little fort near what is now Downend. The locality has been much altered by the reclamation of marshland, by quarrying and by railway and road cuttings, but remains of ancient earthworks can still be traced. It was a bleak, inhospitable haven. We read that 'hunger, fear and 'cold' compelled the Danes to surrender. Not lack of water; there was plenty of that. But it *would* be cold out there on the exposed marshes in early May.

So Alfred received their surrender and made his treaty with them while his men guarded the camp till all was settled, and meantime they helped themselves to the piles of booty which the Danes had collected. In short, they stayed on the Poldens, and to them in due course came Guthrum, the Danish king, to be baptised at Aller and entertained at Wedmore, both of which lie within a few miles.

By this interpretation the campaign reveals coherence. It is much more credible than that Alfred should have spent his time shuttling backwards and forwards between the Somerset marshes and Chippenham.

Regarding the baptism of Guthrum, there is likely to have been some element of superstitious awe in his conversion. The levies whom Alfred met in Selwood could not have been the only people who regarded him as one risen from the dead. That, and the capture of the Raven, must have convinced Guthrum that he was up against a force stronger than he possessed. Also he was doubtless under pressure from the peace party in Mercia and East Anglia. When all was settled, he was allowed to withdraw his forces to Chippenham. From there, in the following year, he retreated to Cirencester and thence to East Anglia where, says *The Chronicle*, 'they settled and divided the land.' Guthrum fades from the scene. There is no suggestion that he did not keep his word.

As mentioned earlier, there was, of course, another faction among the Danes, composed of young hotheads who were spoiling for a fight and had not yet won their fortunes. These, says *The Chronicle*, assembled at Fulham, on the Thames, but after a year they crossed the sea to Frankland. The victory of Wessex was the signal for catastrophe for France and the Low Countries. From 880 onwards *The Anglo-Saxon Chronicle* has so little to record of military events in England that it fills up its pages with summaries of disasters on the Continent. The Franks had a terrible time.

From 878 to 885 profound peace reigned in Wessex. The only encounter with the Danes that is mentioned is a sea-battle off the coast, probably of Kent. King Alfred himself was commanding the English fleet, which attacked four Danish ship-rovers and captured them all. On land it was a period of recovery and reconstruction, at which Alfred proved as gifted as he was in war, as we shall see in our next chapter. In 883 he was able to resume the sending of his annual tribute of Peter's Pence to Rome— though one feels that, at that stage, the money could perhaps have better been used at home.

In 885 the Danes in East Anglia, now presumably under a new leader, broke the treaty with Alfred. He was doubtless expecting it, sooner or later, and was not surprised. Half of the army besieged Rochester, but the citizens held out till Alfred arrived with the West Saxon forces. Then the Danes retired to their ships. In retaliation, and to forestall further trouble, Alfred then sent his own fleet along the coast of East Anglia. At the mouth of the Stour they met 16 Danish ships, captured them and killed all the crews. But on their way back, their ships laden with booty, they met a larger Danish fleet and this time lost the ensuing battle.

Again there was peace in England, and no further trouble with the Danes is reported until 893. Any Viking who yearned for adventure joined the bands which were marauding in Frankland and left the well-defended Wessex severely alone. Alfred, meanwhile, was not idle. In 886, says *The Chronicle*,

he fortified the city of London and committed it to the care of Alderman Ethelred, to hold it under him. And the whole English nation turned to him, except that part of it which was held captive by the Danes.

Alfred's final conflicts with the invaders occupied much of the years 893 to 897. The Danes in this war were under the command of new leaders, Guthrum having died in peace in East Anglia in 890. The name of one of them is given as Haesten. And the account of the war, as provided by *The Anglo-Saxon Chronicle*, is amusing in a way, owing to the literary style of the compiler. Until this time *The Chronicle* had evidently been prepared from older records. It gives the bare bones of events, is terse and concise. But, Alfred having decreed that *The Chronicle* should be copied and kept up-to-date, the writer in the 880s and 890s is a contemporary of the events recorded and perhaps an eye-witness of some of them. He is verbose and repetitious. He wanders off on a long, involved account of a campaign, then suddenly switches back to the beginning, with a phrase or two of explanation. He uses the pronoun 'they' so indiscriminately that it is sometimes difficult to decide whether he is referring to the Danes or the English. Nevertheless, when his sentences are unravelled they are highly informative and provide us with a wealth of first-hand detail.

The events of the war may be summarised as follows. In 893, 250 Danish ships sailed into an inlet in Kent, said to be the Limne river, which probably means an inlet of Romney Marsh, near Lympne. The crews towed their ships four miles inland, 'as far as the Weald', captured a small fort and camped at Appledore. Soon afterwards Haesten with 80 ships entered the mouth of the Thames and made a camp at Milton— which is probably either the Milton near Sittingbourne or the Milton near Gravesend. The chronicler says they were joined by numbers of men from East Anglia and Northumbria who, despite their undertaking to King Alfred, couldn't resist joining in when there was plunder to be had.

Faced with this challenge, Alfred assembled an army somewhere in The Weald, on a site 'defended by wood and by water', where he could keep an eye on both sets of trouble-makers. From their camps the Danes sent out raiding-parties most days, and the English sent detachments to try to catch them. Alfred had devised a system whereby half his army was in the field and half back at their homes, so that they were able to cope with the prolonged skirmishing. In due course, one Danish army (it is not clear which) considered it had accumulated enough booty and tried to by-pass Alfred and get north of the Thames. Alfred's troops, however, intercepted them at Farnham, thoroughly beat them and recovered their booty. Some of the Danes managed to cross the Thames and retreated to an island in the river Colne near Iver, Buckinghamshire. There the English troops besieged them.

Meanwhile, the other army had also decamped and made its way by sea to Devonshire. There it split into two parts, one of them rounding Land's End and attacking north Devon, while the other besieged Exeter. Alfred himself took charge of the English army which hurried to deal with the Danes in Devon, leaving about half his forces, under his son Edward, to cope with those north of the Thames. The sequel was stalemate on both fronts. Edward had not sufficient forces to storm the river island, while the Danes in Exeter gave Alfred the slip and escaped. The Danes with all their scattered fleets and armies then made a rendezvous at Benfleet in Essex.

There they settled behind an earthwork that Haesten had constructed and sent out raiding-parties to collect plunder wherever they could.

One day, when Haesten was away, the English army in eastern Wessex —presumably under the command of Edward—stormed the camp, destroyed the earthworks and captured everything inside it—'money, women and children', says The Chronicle, including Haestens' wife and two sons. The English towed all the ships they could upstream to London and burned the rest. The captives and treasure were also brought to London, but King Alfred, with more chivalry than the Vikings ever showed, returned Haesten's wife and children to him because, says The Chronicle, one of the boys was his godson, having been a hostage at an earlier stage.

When Haesten returned from his raid he collected the scattered forces in Essex and retreated to a new base at Shoebury, farther down the river. There he was joined by more pirates, from East Anglia and Northumbria, obviously willing to resume their old way of life. When he had assembled a sufficiently large force he embarked upon one of those astoundingly rapid and audacious raids so characteristic of the Vikings. The whole army sped up the Thames, spreading devastation, crossed the Cotswolds and then proceeded northwards up the Severn. Ethelred, the alderman of Mercia, together with English troops from all over Wessex (except Devonshire, where Alfred himself was dealing with more trouble) followed hard on their heels and caught up with them at Buttington, near Welshpool, where they besieged them on an island in the Severn. The siege lasted for several weeks until the Danes, having already eaten all their horses, were suffering from famine. In desperation they broke out and cut their way through the besieging English. Although *The Chronicle* claims the battle as a victory, it is obvious that large numbers of Danes managed to escape and, making their way across country, eventually arrived back at Shoebury.

The Vikings were incorrigible and irrepressible. No sooner had they gathered in the stragglers than they were planning another major raid. Strong reinforcements came down from the Danes in Northumbria, and this time Haesten sent his wife, children and treasure deep into the interior of East Anglia. Then, striking across country to Watling Street, the army marched 'at a stretch, day and night', to Chester, where they shut themselves in behind the old Roman walls before the English had realised what was happening. But again the vigour and vigilance of the English army trapped them. Alfred's reorganisation of his forces was proving eminently efficient. The besiegers were evidently not strong enough to prevent the Danes from making sallies and raids, but they adopted a scorched-earth policy which proved very effective. They rounded up all the local cattle, harvested or burned all the corn within easy reach of Chester and cut off any Danish stragglers who ventured outside the city.

Thus thwarted, the Danes turned in the only direction possible and organised raids into North Wales. The Welsh chronicle, *The Annals of the Britons*, records that 'the Northmen came and devastated Loycr, and Brycheiniog, and Gwent and Gwynllywiog' at about this time, which indicates that the raids were fairly extensive, extending into South Wales. Then, realising they had collected all the booty they were likely to acquire, the army escaped into Danish Northumbria and so was able, by traversing friendly territory, to return to Shoebury without molestation.

Back in Essex, they moved their base to Mersea Island, but in the autumn of 894 they brought their ships up the Thames to within a few miles of London and then towed them up the river Lea. An attack on their new camp, about 20 miles up-river, by the citizens of London (who were evidently numerous enough to mount an operation on their own) was repulsed, and stalemate followed. At harvest-time a strong force of English troops guarded the fields around London so that the corn could be safely harvested. One day, the king, on a tour of inspection, spotted a place where an obstruction could be thrown across the river, making it impossible for the Danes to extricate their ships. This was quickly done, and a fort built on either side of the river to protect the barrier. Realising how they had again been trapped, the Danes broke camp, sent their women and children into East Anglia and themselves embarked on another marathon march across country. Again they made for the Severn, probably following Watling Street as before, and before the English could catch up with them had dug themselves in at a place called Quatbridge (now Bridgnorth). There they stayed all the winter, watched by the vigilant English, but at last, in the following summer, gave up in despair.

The Army had been outmanouvred, harassed and checkmated. The English defences, created by Egbert, maintained by Ethelwulf and his sons and now brilliantly developed and operated by Alfred, had proved a match for an enemy who had over-run far more powerful kingdoms on the Continent. The Danes had used their whole repertoire—frontal attacks, diversionary moves, attacks by sea, incredibly swift marches overland, treachery, assaults by night, attacks in midwinter, the sudden breaking of treaties—but nothing had succeeded. This was not the sort of campaign they enjoyed; while they revelled in a good fight, they liked it to be followed by an orgy of plunder. In England over the past few years they had had too much fighting and not nearly enough plunder.

In the summer of 896 the Army at last dispersed. Some settled in East Anglia and Northumbria and, says *The Chronicle*, 'those that were penniless got themselves ships and went south over the sea to the Seine.' The great ordeal was over at last. For the remaining four years of Alfred's reign his only trouble with the Vikings consisted of pirate raids along the south coast. *The Chronicle* gives details of one such raid, in the course of which six Danish ships appeared first off the Isle of Wight, then went on to raid Devonshire and were brought to bay. In the sea-shore battle three ships were destroyed and their crews killed. The others, badly damaged, limped along as far as the Sussex coast but were then driven ashore. The English troops rounded up the crews and brought them to Winchester, where Alfred ordered them all to be hanged. Only one ship, with a crew of badly wounded men, escaped back to East Anglia.

For in containing the Viking menace at sea Alfred was as successful as he had been on land. *The Anglo-Saxon Chronicle* records that the Danish pirates relied on their ships of traditional type, called *esks*.

Then King Alfred gave orders for building long ships against the *esks*, which were full-nigh twice as long as the others. Some had sixty oars, some more; and they were both swifter and steadier and also higher than the others. They were not shaped either after the Friesian or the Danish model but so as he himself thought that they might be most serviceable.

What a versatile genius this Alfred was. England's greatest king, he died in 901 (according to *The Anglo-Saxon Chronicle;* 899 by a modern reckoning) 'six nights before the mass of All Saints'. He died peacefully, in a realm at peace. Impressive though his campaigns were, they were easily surpassed by his work in the reconstruction of England and by the vision he brought to the task. Of this we read in the next chapter. But perhaps not the least of his achievements was the training of a worthy son-and-heir who consolidated and continued what he had begun.

VIII

The Character
and Achievements of Alfred

In the annals of those distant days few human figures stand out with any clarity. The chronicles tend to be catalogues of major events in which most of the players are little more than names. Attempts to assess their character are essays in speculation, based on slender clues.

Among the few of whom sufficient details are recorded to enable us to *know* the man, Alfred is outstanding. We, in an age of widespread education, established law and order, innate humanity, appreciation of the arts, and a questing zeal that seeks to probe the unknown, peer back through the dim centuries and discern, amid the mindless barbarism and chaos, the towering figure of a man like ourselves. Dressed in twentieth-century clothes and given the benefits of our own education and background, he would stand equal to the best minds of our age. Above all, he is a thoughtful man, and we can follow his thought processes. We can identify ourselves with him as he thinks through his stupendous problems—weighing, calculating, deciding, sometimes making mistakes but never giving in. And some of his decisions were undoubtedly more enlightened and humane than some of ours would have been under the same circumstances.

As with all men, environment played an important part in the development of Alfred's character. He was evidently reared against the background of a happy family-life. Both his father and his mother were 'good' people. His father, Ethelwulf, appears as a kindly, deeply religious man, though not always a paragon of wisdom. Osburga, his wife, seems to have been an ideal mother, devoted to her children. In the well-known story, preserved by Asser, we see her also as a lover of beautiful things and of the stirring cadences of Saxon poetry. Asser relates how Osburga showed her sons a book of poems with ornate lettering and beautiful painted binding, and promised to give it to the one who could first recite to her the verses it

87

contained. (It was *not*, by the way, a prize for reading but for learning the poems by heart.) Alfred, then apparently only about four years old, easily won the award—though possibly his elder brothers did not try. An interesting incidental possibility is that Osburga herself may have been able to read it, which would have been a most unusual accomplishment for a woman in those days, when literacy was rare.

A little speculation may here be not only permissible but profitable. Here we have a devout king, Ethelwulf, who in his youth had definite leanings towards entering the church and who, if he could have chosen, would probably have done so. He has three grown-up sons, a daughter married to a neighbouring king, and one small boy, 14 years younger than the next of the family. The boy is proving to be highly intelligent, even precocious, and with a liking for books and art rather unusual in a noble family. What is the obvious decision of such a father in such circumstances? To prepare the boy to enter the Church; what else is there for him in life? With three energetic elder brothers, he cannot hope to inherit a kingdom, but he has the makings of a good bishop. Perhaps he will one day become Bishop of Winchester or Archbishop of Canterbury and be a pillar of strength to whichever of his brothers is occupying the throne.

Shortly afterwards, according to one reckoning when the boy was still only four, Ethelwulf sent him to Rome. It seems an extraordinary thing to do, although the young prince was accompanied by an ample retinue and shown every hospitality *en route*, by order of Charles, King of the Franks. Here, as in so many other matters, Ethelwulf was evidently following the precedent set by Charlemagne, who sent his sons to receive the Papal benediction. After Pope Leo had, at the coronation ceremony in 800, taken the crown and placed it on Charlemagne's head the tradition seems to have quickly grown that the Pope had mystical authority which placed him above the Emperor. The astute Charlemagne, though taken aback by the Pope's action at the time, soon realised that to have the spiritual backing of the Church gave him a strong advantage and so fostered the idea.

Something similar seems to have been in Ethelwulf's mind. It is said that the Pope took Alfred and adopted him as his spiritual son. One tradition says that he anointed the boy king, but that seems unlikely. More probably this anointing was a kind of consecration—a kind of baptism which it was hoped would eventually bear fruits in a life devoted to the Church. It is not impossible that the doting Ethelwulf saw in his favourite son a possible future Pope.

Two years later, still only six years old, Alfred made the long journey to Rome again. This time his father went with him. It was a royal progress, the King of the Franks, Charles, again providing an impressive escort through his kingdom. In Rome they spent a whole year. We have noted earlier (page 61) the lavish gifts which Ethelwulf presented to the Pope. He had already created a good impression by presenting, before leaving England, a tenth of his private property to the Church, and in Rome he rebuilt the Saxon school, founded by King Ina and since destroyed by fire, and endowed it with extreme generosity. He also contracted to send annually to Rome, from his private purse, 300 marks, of which 100 were to be a personal present for the Pope. From this undertaking arose the tradition of the collection of 'Peter's Pence', so unpopular in England in later centuries. But whatever the feelings in England, Ethelwulf must certainly have been popular in Rome.

Incidentally, in the years of comparative tranquillity which followed the Peace of Wedmore, Alfred honoured his father's contract by resuming the annual contribution to Rome. Beginning in 883, *The Anglo-Saxon Chronicle*, evidently somewhat short on other material, records the sending of the tribute and the names of the messengers who delivered it. In one year the emissary was 'Alderman Beeke'; in another, 'Abbot Bernhelm'; and in 889 'there was no journey to Rome, except that King Alfred sent two messengers with letters'. The entry for the year 883 contains the intriguing and startling information that Sighelm and Athelstan took the alms to Rome 'and also in India to St. Thomas and St. Bartholomew'. It is true that there was, and still is, a Thomasine church in southern India, but was Alfred in touch with these distant Christians?

How Alfred spent the year in Rome is not recorded. No doubt there were other young princes from other countries in the Eternal City, and there may have been arrangements for bringing them together. It is tempting to assume that they went to school together or at least had private tutors, but perhaps not, for it is recorded that Alfred did not learn to read till he was twelve years old and that in the 880s, when settling the kingdom after the ebbing of the Danish tide, he was still struggling to learn Latin. What is certain is that the sights and sounds of Rome must have made a considerable impact on his impressionable mind. For ever afterwards he must have measured Wessex against the sophistication and civilisation that he tasted there. It was this which made his fight against the barbarism represented by the Danes worthwhile. Here was the model for the state which in his later years he endeavoured to establish in England. That he could never fully succeed in his lifetime he knew, but at least he could lay the foundations. His genius was in being able to distinguish which were essentials and which the spurious overlay.

For all his great qualities, Alfred was no saint. One tradition, perpetuated in an anonymous *Life of St. Neot*, says that in his youth Alfred was arrogant and high-handed, tending to reject complaints and petitions brought to him. He was warned by St. Neot to mend his ways, as in an approaching time of disaster he too would be brought low and would need himself to ask favours. Alfred scornfully rejected the warning, but later, in exile in the Somerset marshes, recognised the justice of the rebuke and came back to his kingdom a changed man. The story cannot be entirely true, as St. Neot lived in a later age, but the gist of it may be accurate. With it is connected the popular story of Alfred and the burnt cakes. There is a suggestion that this tale survived through being made into a popular song, which seems likely enough. A speech put into the mouth of the herdsman's wife when she finds that Alfred, whom she took to be another serf, had allowed her cakes to burn, looks like a fragment of a ballad:

Holla, companion!
Dost not see that the bread there is burning? Why lazily sit and not turn it?
Ready enough thou wilt be to take it from us and devour it.

Florence of Worcester, a writer of the early twelfth century, relates an allied tradition concerning the elevation of one Denewulf to the bishopric of Winchester:

This man, if we may trust the report, at his advanced age had not acquainted with the art of reading, and in his early days had been a swineherd. When Alfred lived in exile in the forests, he became acquainted with Denewulf as he was driving his swine to the oak-woods to feed on acorns. The natural talents of the man interested the king, who took pains with his instruction, and afterwards promoted him to a high dignity.

Tradition, of course, identified Denewulf with the husband of the cottage wife who scolded the king.

The stories are not improbable. Willingness to acknowledge mistakes and to alter their ways have been the hallmark of great men through the ages. It could well be that the hardships of life as a fugitive taught the king to appreciate the true value of men, regardless of rank and appearance.

Another popular story of the months of exile is, of course, the one about Alfred penetrating into the heart of the Danish camp disguised as a minstrel and so learning of their plans. Similar stories are, however, told of other heroes in Norse legends. Perhaps the most significant aspect of the tradition is that the chroniclers readily accepted that that was the sort of thing that Alfred would have done. It is a tribute to his courage and resource, and also to his love of the old heroic songs of which the Saxons and the Danes enjoyed a common heritage.

Evidence of Alfred's deep religious feelings may be seen in his insistence that his antagonist, Guthrum, be baptised after the battle of Ethandune. We cannot know how Guthrum's acquiesence was achieved, but the Danes must have been impressed and overawed by the way in which Alfred had turned an almost complete defeat into an even more conclusive victory. To them there must have seemed something supernatural about it. We can, perhaps, permit ourselves to imagine Alfred assuring Guthrum that he was indeed trying to match himself against an unconquerable God, and Guthrum, convinced by the course of events of the truth of this, resolving that if he couldn't beat these Christians he would join them. The fact that he now intended to go back and settle down to a more peaceful life in East Anglia, where conceivably the Christian deity might be of more use to him than the restless war-gods of the North, may also have weighed with him. Whatever the cogent arguments on either side, there can be no doubt that Alfred put a high value on Guthrum's conversion.

It has been claimed that Alfred was a ruthless man, that there are no traditions illustrating his mercy. If that were so, there would be ample excuse in the atrocities that the Danes had inflicted on England. The records, however, show him as a man of moderation. Even when, as noted on page 85, he captured two shiploads of Danes (who, after all, were pirates) off Selsey and had them brought to Winchester for execution, he sentenced them to the relatively merciful death of hanging and not, as was commonplace in those days, by mutilation or burning. Even today there is to be seen on a church-door in Herefordshire a fragment of darkish substance said to be a piece of a Dane's skin, probably removed from him when he was still alive and nailed there by parishioners who had suffered equally horrifying treatment at the hands of Danes.

When Guthrum left Wessex he went not only bearing gifts which Alfred had given him but also with the knowledge that he was retreating to a territory over which his conqueror laid no claim. A more ambitious man than Alfred would have tried to annex the whole of the lands occupied by the Danes in the East and North, thus increasing his troubles, but Alfred knew how to compromise, and doubtless he also understood his limitations. To the very end this modest man never claimed on the documents he signed to be more than 'The King of the West Saxons', though *The Anglo-Saxon Chronicle* records, 'the whole English nation turned to him, except that part of it which was held captive by the Danes'. The boundary between the English and Danish kingdoms, as agreed by Alfred and Guthrum, followed the mouth of the Thames westwards to the junction with the river Lea; then up the Lea to its source; then in a straight line to Bedford; and from thence along the river Ouse to Watling

Street, which served as a frontier to the mouth of the Dee. To the east lay Danish-controlled territory, some under Guthrum and some under other kings.

To the west the truncated kingdom of Mercia imposed a buffer-zone between the Danelaw, as the Danish territories were termed, and Wessex.

Now until it had been over-run by the Danes in the early 870s, Mercia had been an important independent kingdom. The last king recorded in *The Chronicle* is the puppet Ceolwulf, appointed by the Danes in 874. After the Peace of Wedmore, however, it seems that Alfred appointed a nominee of his own, Ethelred, to govern the country. Ethelred was content with the title 'Alderman of Mercia'. His loyalty to Alfred was unswerving, though he led the Mercian armies into battle and presided over the Mercian Council. In age he seems to have been a young man, perhaps a little older than Alfred's son Edward. He married Alfred's eldest daughter, Ethelfleda, later to be known as 'The Lady of the Mercians', in about 887 when he was probably in his early twenties.

In 883 Alfred and the armies of Wessex 'sat against the Army at London; and there, with the favour of God, they were very successful, after the performance of their vows'. The wording seems to indicate a siege and considerable fighting. Three years later we read that Alfred fortified London: 'He then committed the city to the care of Alderman Ethelred, to hold it under him.' London thus became a strong frontier fortress, designed for the specific purpose of keeping the Danes in check. It also kept open the Thames for the Continental trade for which it was the most convenient port. In handing it over to Ethelred Alfred displayed clever statesmanship. He had given the city back to Mercia, to which it traditionally belonged, but at the same time he had installed a thoroughly reliable and able young man to hold it for him. Thereafter London, which had experienced several centuries of obscurity, began to flourish and grow. Alfred may be credited with being the true founder of its prosperity.

One senses, too, that Alfred well knew how to delegate authority. He surrounded himself with energetic young men and, when he judged them ready, gave them responsibility and let them exercise it. Edward his son, Ethelred his son-in-law, Ethelm, Wulfric, Ethelnoth and the rest were quite capable of collecting the local levies and engaging the Danes as required.

London was only one of about 25 burghs (later to become towns) which Alfred fortified, some on the sites of old Roman cities but most as entirely new foundations. To what extent in his military organisation Alfred was expanding on the work of his grandfather Egbert and to what extent he was initiating a new system is uncertain. The appointment of aldermen, each to lead the fyrd, or citizen army, of a shire seems to have derived from Egbert and to have served Alfred quite well. But Egbert's strategy was not designed specifically against the Danes, whose menace had not developed in his time; he probably had more in mind the normal differences of opinion between his kingdom and his neighbours, both English and Welsh. Alfred, on the other hand, had no doubts about his chief enemy.

The superiority of the Vikings lay largely in their mobility. When the Saxons could bring them to bay and engage in a straight battle, they beat them as often as not; but the Danes could strike anywhere, either by sea or by one of their astonishing cross-country raids on stolen horses. It was impossible for the Saxons to guard every land-frontier and every bay, river or other landing-point on the coast. To meet the challenge on land, Alfred devised a system of fortified burghs or boroughs. Ideally he wanted one in every district, so that at the first alarm the local inhabitants could take refuge there. Each burgh was fortified, though not on any lavish scale, for the impoverished countryside could not afford it. But it had a permanent garrison, for every local thane had either to build a house inside its walls and live in it or to delegate that responsibility to a fighting-man whom he had to support. Alfred's realm thus became studded with strong-points where the people could rally when the alarm was sounded. Most of the burghs thus founded lived on to become important towns in later centuries. And, as we note in a later chapter, Alfred's successors extended the principle throughout the Midlands.

Regarding the defences of the coast, as already observed Alfred constructed a fleet consisting of larger vessels than those of the enemy. Although they may not have been able to cope with a full invasion fleet, they were quite capable of dealing with even large-scale pirate raids, such as the one which led to the capture of the two ship-loads of Danes off Selsey in 896.

The efficacy of Alfred's defence measures was proved by the failure of the Danish invasion in 893–6. The concerted attacks, by sea and land, which were of the same sort that not quite 20 years earlier had been overwhelming, achieved next to nothing. The Danes captured some plunder, and lost it again. They chased around the coast and across the country by the Roman highways and accomplished little except a large mileage. When it was all over many of them, according to *The Chronicle*, had to try for better luck on the Continent, for they finished their long campaign penniless.

Efficient though Alfred was as an army commander and military strategist, this was not where his heart lay. His love was for art, music, literature and science. He dreamed of a land at peace in which all these flowers of civilisation would bloom, and his task, as he saw it, was the creation or restoration of such a state. In the grimmest and most anxious times much of his thoughts were occupied with plans for reconstruction. And in the intervals of his campaign, when he was actually in the field, he would have monks to read to him or minstrels to sing him the old Saxon lays. This self-disciplined man even devised a candle-clock to enable him better to divide the day between his numerous interests.

Alfred rightly saw that the fabric of the realm he was building must be founded on sound laws, impartially applied. He therefore collected all the codified laws then in existence in England—notably those of Ina of Wessex, Offa of Mercia, and Ethelbert of Kent—together with evidence of existing common law, and, by a process of selection, fashioned them into a code for use throughout his domain. Though fairly conservative in content, Alfred's code was an improvement on its predecessors. It limited the blood-feud, which was rampant, defined the sundry services which a man owed to his lord, was strong in the protection of church personnel and property, insisted on the proper observance of holy days, and was biassed in favour of the weak and underprivileged against oppression.

Traditionally, local courts, presided over by local lords, aldermen or thanes, administered justice and meted out punishments. In the chaos of the Danish wars the holding of regular courts had lapsed in many districts, and the dispensation of justice had become a matter of chance. Alfred not only restored the courts but insisted that they functioned as they were meant to.

He still followed the traditional practice of journeying around his kingdom, staying for a few days here and a few there—until local food supplies gave out. This gave him the opportunity to keep in touch with what was going on. Having settled in for a short sojourn at a royal manor he would send for the record-book to check on the activities of the local courts. All decisions, says Asser, were submitted to him, and he investigated them strictly to see whether they were just or unjust. He also encouraged his staff to inform him of any miscarriages of justice, especially if bribery or malice were involved. Then the unjust judge had to appear and explain his conduct to Alfred, who made no allowances even for ignorance. According to Asser, his admonition to such a judge ran:

I am astonished at your great temerity that you, who by God's favour and mine, have been entrusted with the office and rank of 'The Wise', should have entirely neglected the studies and labours of The Wise. Either, therefore, resign your temporal power or apply yourself, as I require you, to obtain wisdom.

The imperfect judges took heed. In all the records after Ethandune Alfred appears as the unquestioned and undisputed master.

'It was a strange sight,' writes Asser,

to see the Aldermen, who were almost illiterate from infancy, and the reeves and other officials learning how to read, preferring this unaccustomed and laborious discipline to losing the exercises of their power.

One has an increasing respect for Alfred.

He rightly attached great importance to literacy. In the preface to one of his books he sets down his thoughts on the matter, revealing also how he viewed his kingdom and contrasting it with a past which may not have been quite such a golden age as he visualised:

Alfred the king bids greet Waerferth the bishop with his words, lovingly and in a friendly way; and I bid you to know that it has very often come to my mind what wise men there once were throughout England, men of both holy and of wordly wisdom, and how happy the times were then throughout England . . . and how successful they were both in war and in wisdom; and also the men of the church, how eager they were both about learning and about teaching, and about the laws of service that they should do for God; and how men came hither to this land from overseas to seek wisdom and learning; and we now should seek these from outside if we should have them. Learning in England was fallen so clean away that there were very few this side of the Humber who could understand their services in English, or, furthermore, who could translate a written message from Latin into English —and I think that there were not many beyond the Humber. So few were there, that I cannot think of any single one south of the Thames when I took the kingdom. Thanks be to Almighty God that we now have any supply of teachers. . . .

When I called this to mind I remembered how I had seen, before it was all harried and burned, how the churches throughout all England stood filled with treasures and books, and also how very many were the servants of God, and yet they knew very little of how to use these books. . . .

With this preamble, he ordered his bishops that

all the sons of freemen who have the means to undertake it should be set to learning English letters, and such as are fit for a more advanced education and are intended for high office should be taught Latin also.

If this programme was implemented, and we may be sure that as far as possible it was, the part of England that was under the control of Alfred must have been the most literate country in Europe. We remember that only just before Alfred's time the great Emperor Charlemagne could hardly sign his name. And Alfred's insistence on the use of English as a written language is remarkable, in an age when most documents and literature were written in Latin. He must be regarded as one of the

4A

fathers of English literature. For this astonishing man, not content with being a scholar and insisting that all of his subjects capable of doing so should also be scholars, now determined to provide his people with some English literature to read. In the last seven or eight years of his reign he translated five major Latin works into English. They were Pope Gregory's *Cura Pastoralis* (Pastoral Care), Orosius's *History of the World*, Bede's *Ecclesiastical History*, St. Augustine's *Soliloquies*, and Boethius's *Consolations of Philosophy*. For him Gregory's *Pastoral Care* set out admirably his own programme of education, for it emphasised to his bishops their responsibility for teaching the laymen under their care. Alfred sent a copy of his translation to each of his bishops.

One of the books which must have appealed to him most was Boethius's *Consolations of Philosophy*. It describes the thoughts of a king who, by a sudden change of furtune, has been toppled from his throne and is now in a miserable dungeon awaiting a probably humiliating and painful execution. The king comes to the conclusion that, to the philosophic mind, 'the slings and arrows of outrageous fortune' are irrelevant, especially to those who are sustained by the Christian faith. For Alfred it could almost have been autobiography.

Orosius deals with the history of the ancient world, but to it Alfred adds some original investigations of his own, in his conversation with the Norse sea-captain, Ohthere:

Ohthere told his lord King Alfred that he dwelt northmost of all the Northmen. . . . He said that that land is very long north from thence, but it is all waste, except in a few places, where the Finns here and there dwell, for hunting in the winter, and in summer for fishing in that sea. He said that he was desirous to try, once upon a time, how far that country extended due north, or whether anyone lived to the north of the waste. He then went due north along the country, leaving all the way waste land on the right, and the wide sea on the left, for three days; he was as far north as the whale-hunters go at the farthest. Then he proceeded in his course due north, as far as he could sail within another three days; then the land there inclined due east, or the sea into the land, he knew not which, but he knew that there he waited for a west wind, or a little north, and sailed thence eastward along that land, as far as he could sail in four days. Then he had to wait for a north wind, because the land there inclined due south, or the sea in on that land, he knew not which. He then sailed thence along the coast due south, as far as he could sail in five days. There lay a great river in that land. They then turned up in that river; because they durst not sail on that river, on account of hostility, because all that country was inhabited on the other side of that river. . . . The Beormas had well cultivated their country, but they did not dare to enter it. . . .

Ohthere had, in fact, rounded the North Cape and had discovered the

White Sea. The account he gives is our first glimpse of those northern regions, and we are grateful to Alfred's questing mind for recording it. It is very unlikely that he wrote down his books himself. More probably he dictated them to scribes, discussing them sentence by sentence with the learned men he had gathered around him. One of these was Bishop Asser, whom he tempted from the monastery of St. David's and who afterwards wrote his biography. Others known by name were Plegmund, Archbishop of Canterbury; Werfrith, Bishop of Worcester; Grimbold, a monk from a monastery at St. Omer; and a continental Saxon named John, whom he made abbot of the abbey he found at Athelney.

In addition to the translations in which he was personally involved Alfred was, of course, responsible for the revision of that great work, *The Anglo-Saxon Chronicle*. In order that there should be no danger of it ever being irretrievably lost he decreed that copies be placed in all the great cathedral churches and chief monasteries and be kept up-to-date. Due to these measures it has survived all the vicissitudes of subsequent ages, and we still have copies written by the hands of scholars who were alive in Alfred's day.

To find time for all the things he wanted to do, Alfred worked out a timetable whereby half his hours, including both day and night, were occupied in secular matters and half devoted to the service of God. He likewise divided his income into half—one-half for himself and one-half for God. Of God's half, a fifth was devoted to the poor, two-fifths to two monasteries he had founded, one-fifth to other monasteries, and one-fifth to a school. With his own half he was similarly generous, giving one-third for entertaining overseas visitors, one-third for builders, sculptors and artisans engaged in his reconstruction works, and one-third for his ministers, scholars and household expenses. He seems to have kept very little money for himself.

Asser seems to imply that Alfred's ministers were at times an argumentative lot. No doubt they had their full share of stubborn Saxon independence—or, as some would call it, pig-headedness. Alfred had frequently to soothe ruffled feelings.

His family life, however, seems to have been happy. The good relations which prevailed among the brothers (with the possible exception of Ethelbald) in his father's household were duplicated in his own. His wife, Elswitha, took no part in politics or public affairs but contented herself with domestic duties and rearing her children. She was with Alfred in his months of exile and lost several of her children in infancy, perhaps owing in part to the hardships she endured.

The eldest surviving child of the family was Ethelfleda who, as we have seen, married Ethelred, alderman of Mercia. A lady of extraordinary strength of character, she inherited many of her father's characteristics and carried on his work vigorously in Mercia after her husband's death. Edward, the eldest son, was a warrior rather than a scholar, though in that capacity he probably took a good deal of weight from his father's shoulders. The relationship between father and son seems to have been amicable. After Edward came two daughters, Ethelgeda and Elfrida. Ethelgeda is said to have been delicate and may have been deformed or lame. Expecting never to get married, she entered a nunnery and became Abbess of Shaftesbury, a position she held to her death. Elfrida married Count Baldwin of Flanders who, incidentally, was the son of Judith, the little Frankish princess whose first husband was Ethelwulf.

There was one other son, Ethelward, the youngest of the family, who inherited his father's love of scholarship and literature. During his lifetime he was regarded as crown prince and signed documents as such, but he died before his brother Edward.

In his will, which survives, Alfred left ample provision for all the members of his family, including considerable sums of money to his wife and children and a sword valued at 120 marks (an enormous sum in those days) to his son-in-law Ethelred. He also left handsome legacies to his advisers, retainers, bishops and other friends, as well as money for sundry churches, priests and the needy poor. He ensured that all the estates and personal property that had belonged to his brother Ethelred, who had died in 871 leaving two infant sons, should go to those sons, Ethelhelm and Ethelwald. Finally, he decreed that all bond-men in his possession should be given their freedom. It was a will worthy of Alfred—scrupulously fair and meticulous in every detail.

He died on 26 October 899, probably at Winchester. The cause of his death is not known, but probably, at the age of fifty, he was worn out by the hardships and exertions of his strenuous life. From childhood, however, he had suffered from a distressing illness which attacked suddenly at irregular intervals. One inconvenient occasion was at his wedding feast in 868, when his sudden agony put a stop to the festivities. Asser recounts stories of Alfred praying that God would relieve him of his malady, replacing it, if necessary, by something less debilitating—though, he added, not one which would unfit him for his royal duties in the eyes of men, such as blindness or leprosy, of which he lived in dread. Asser, probably exaggerating, also says that for 20 years (up to the time when he was writing) Alfred had

suffered continual and severe attacks from an obscure illness, so that he has not had a moment's relief, either from the pain caused by the illness nor from the depression from which he suffers in anticipation of an attack.

Elsewhere, however, he says that when Alfred could rest 'for a night or a day or even an hour' he would recover and carry on with his work. Still, the fear of an attack was always there, and the pain must have worn him down.

It is salutary to recognise that the prodigious achievements of this great man were made against a background of illness and physical weakness.

€dward

Edward was a soldier—brave, efficient and uncomplicated. Not for him the scholarly studies, the devotion to the Church, the multifarious interests of his mighty father. He was entirely a man of action—a man's man—and as such he must have been readily acceptable to a generation of warriors brought up in the hard school of the Danish wars. Alfred himself undoubtedly appreciated this. While he was delighted in his younger son, Ethelward, who had obviously inherited his love for literature and learning, he must have known that the country needed a strong character like young Edward. So he made sure that the lad received a sound military training and was given responsibility as soon as he was able to take it.

Edward was probably born about the year 870. In that year of trials, 878, he must therefore have been eight or nine. Doubtless he experienced the hasty flight from Chippenham and shared in the hardships of life in the Somerset woods and marshes. When the next formidable irruption of the Danes occurred, in 892 and 893, he was old enough to take command of a section of the army. It was he and his men who caught the Danish raiders, laden with booty, at Farnham, thoroughly routed them and chased them across country to the Thames, later besieging them on the island of Thorney, in the river Coln.

The West Saxons, therefore, were used to being led by Edward. After the death of his brother Ethelward, it was taken for granted that he would in due course succeed his father. When, in October, 899, death at last claimed Alfred, Edward automatically took over the kingdom.

His accession was, however, not uneventful. When King Ethelred had died of wounds or exhaustion at Wimborne in 871 he had left two infant sons. By the rights of primogeniture, which were not strictly followed in the Anglo-Saxon kingdoms, they of course had prior claim to the throne. With the Danes over-running the kingdom, no-one would have been so

foolish as to put forward a small child as king, and Alfred had been
accepted without question, nor was his right to the throne ever challenged
during his lifetime. He was evidently scrupulously fair in his dealings with
his nephews and, as we have seen, in his will confirmed them in possession
of all their private hereditary estates.

With this the elder brother, Ethelhelm, was evidently content. He was a
scholarly, unambitious man, much like his father and his grandfather,
Ethelwulf. His younger brother, Ethelwald, was a more difficult character.
We can perhaps see him as a man with a chip on his shoulder, resentful of
the status of the house of Alfred. On Alfred's death he collected a band of
followers and occupied the royal estates at Wimborne and Twineham
(Christchurch). Edward reacted swiftly. 'That same night' he appeared
with his army outside Wimborne, where Ethelwald had barricaded himself
in, and camped in the old Iron Age earthwork of Badbury Rings. Ethelwald
sent messages of defiance, declaring that in Wimborne he would live or
die, after which 'he stole away in the night', leaving his followers, except
the few who accompanied him, to make the best terms they could. Edward
gave orders for a detachment of his army to ride after him, but they could
not overtake him. They did, however, catch up with Ethelwald's wife who,
says *The Chronicle*, was a consecrated nun, 'whom Ethelwald had taken
without the king's leave and against the command of the bishops'. Ethelwald was evidently a headstrong young man.

The fugitive escaped to Northumbria, where 'the Danes received him
as their king'. Doubtless they recognised a valuable ally in settling old
scores with Wessex. Two years of comparative peace followed, and then
Ethelwald arrived in Essex with a considerable fleet, apparently gathered
from various quarters. In the next year, 902, he 'enticed the Army in
East Anglia to rebellion'. Evidently the Danes of Northumbria no longer
followed him as their leader, and the use of the word 'rebellion' makes one
wonder whether the Danes of East Anglia were rebelling against their own
king or whether they had already given allegiance to Alfred or Edward.

The campaign began with a raid in typical Danish style:

The Army over-ran all the land of Mercia, until they came to Cricklade,
where they forded the Thames; and having seized, either in Bradon or
thereabouts, all that they could lay their hands upon, they went homeward
again.

A plundering expedition of the usual type.

King Edward went after them, as soon as he could gather his army, and over-
ran all their land between the foss and the Ouse, quite to the fens northward.
Then, being desirous of returning thence, he issued an order through the

whole army, that they should all go out at once. But the Kentish men remained behind, contrary to his order, though he had sent seven messengers to them. Whereupon the Army surrounded them, and there they fought.

The battle was fierce. *The Anglo-Saxon Chronicle* gives a list of the chief men who fell on either side—aldermen, thanes and an abbot on the English side; a king and several 'governors' on the Danish. 'Of the Danes there were more slain, though they remained masters of the field.' In other words, the Danes won, as was to be expected under the circumstances, but the Danish casualties included 'Prince Ethelwald, who had enticed them to the war'.

In the grand panorama of history it was a mere episode. The death of Ethelwald removed a possible future nuisance. Equally important, Edward had demonstrated conclusively, both to his own people and to the Danes, that he could act rapidly and decisively. There were to be no easy pickings for any adventurers in Wessex. A peace treaty was subsequently signed between Edward and the Danes of both East Anglia and Northumbria, at 'Yttingaford'.

War with the Danes was resumed in 909, apparently on the initiative of Edward, though doubtless he was provoked by raids across the border. With a West Saxon and Mercian army he moved into Northumbria and stayed there for five weeks, doing much damage until the Northumbrians agreed to make peace on his terms. Next year they broke the truce. First they sent a fleet southwards along the east coast, with Kent their apparent destination. Edward moved over to Kent to meet the threat and collected about 100 ships, with the idea of intercepting the invaders at sea, 'The Army therefore supposed that the greatest part of his force was in the ships and that they might go, without being attacked, wherever they would'. The northern Danes thereupon embarked on a gigantic plundering raid. They crossed into Mercia and poured southwards, over the Severn and south as far as the Bristol Avon. Their feint with the fleet had been overwhelmingly successful, but the time was past when they could engage in that sort of expedition with impunity; Edward had an army as mobile as theirs. He caught up with their rearguard at Tettenhall, in Staffordshire, as they were retreating with their loot, and gave the Danes one of the worst beatings they ever experienced in all the Danish wars. Thousands of them, including two kings, were killed and much plunder recovered.

The battle of Tettenhall was crucial for the success of the plans which Edward may have already formulated and which he soon afterwards began to put into effect. This was the removal for ever of the threat to Wessex and Mercia by the Danes on the far side of Watling Street. Alfred had fought the Danes to a standstill, but they still held English territory from which they could, when the opportunity offered, launch new attacks. Edward proposed to carry the war into enemy territory and to deprive them of their bases.

In the year after the battle of Tettenhall, Ethelred of Mercia died. He had been the ever-loyal ally of his father-in-law, Alfred, and his brother-in-law, Edward, never seeking to re-establish the independence of Mercia with himself as king but being content with the status of Alderman. The united front which Alfred and Edward were thus enabled to present to the Danes had had much to do with their success. On his death his widow, the redoubtable Ethelfleda, was accepted as his successor, with the title 'Lady of the Mercians'. She must have been a remarkable personality, to have gained and kept control of a country in an almost perpetual state of war with a formidable enemy on its doorstep—but then, she was the daughter of Alfred. She held the reins of government firmly for eight years till her death in 918, planning and leading campaigns against the Danes in close co-operation with her brother Edward. There were no revolts against her.

As a preliminary, Edward himself took over the towns of London and Oxford, to be developed as bases for the campaign against the Danes. He and Ethelfleda then embarked on a programme of expanding Alfred's strategy of building fortress boroughs. Many modern cities and towns owe their origin to these two military strategists and their eye for good defensive positions. The process had already begun in 906 when, after the treaty of Yttingaford, the walls of Chester were rebuilt, while in 911, the year that her husband died, Ethelfleda fortified Bridgnorth. In 912 Edward built two forts, one on either side of the river Lea at Hertford, an ideal base for activities in East Anglia. From there, in early summer, he took part of his army into Essex and built a fort and town at Witham— 'Many of the people submitted to him, who were before under the power of the Danes'. Meanwhile Ethelfleda, having established Bridgnorth as a key-point from which her army could keep an eye on the Welsh, spent the year in a flurry of fortress-building. Those listed in *The Anglo-Saxon Chronicle* are Tamworth, Stafford, Eddisbury, Warwick, Chirbury, Warburton and Runcorn. A study of the map reveals much of the thinking behind the choice of these sites. Tamworth and Stafford are both just beyond Watling Street, in territory left in Danish hands by Alfred's treaties; Eddisbury, Warburton and Runcorn are in Cheshire, commanding crossings of the Mersey but again well inside Danish territory. They evidently represent a gesture to keep the Northumbrian Danes quiet and a safeguard against any repetition of the invasion of two years earlier. Chirbury is in a far western corner of Shropshire, on the border with Powis. Its purpose became apparent in 915, when Ethelfleda launched an army into Wales and 'stormed Brecknock, and there took the king's wife, with some four and thirty others'. The reason for this expedition is said to have been the murder of an English abbot by the Welsh.

In minor fighting in the following year Northampton and Leicester are mentioned as headquarters of the Danish armies, but battles are recorded at Hockerton, in Nottinghamshire and Leighton, in Bedfordshire, both well inside the Danelaw. Then, in 914, Edward had to face a major invasion of the sort that had occurred in his father's day. A great Danish fleet sailed from Britanny and, by way of the Severn, into Wales, where they plundered at will. The Mercian army, however, was soon at their rear, defeating them in a pitched battle in which one of the Danish earls was killed, and then cornering them in 'a park'. The Danes were allowed to leave after giving pledges and hostages, but Edward rightly put little faith in their word and sent contingents of his army to watch them as they sailed down the Severn.

Thwarted in attempts to land elsewhere, the raiders slipped by night first into Watchet and then Porlock, on the north coast of Somerset, but again found the English ready for them: only those who swam out to their ships managed to escape, says *The Chronicle*. Some of the pirates then took refuge on Flatholm, a tiny island in the mouth of the Severn, where 'many men died of hunger, because they could not reach any meat'. Eventually the remnants of the invaders escaped to Ireland.

Edward had proved entirely capable of defending the land his father had bequeathed to him.

Satisfied that the Danes of eastern England could now expect no further help from overseas, Edward resumed his advance there. Before the end of the year he occupied Buckingham and followed the usual course of building a fortress (in this instance, two fortresses) there. Alarmed, the Danish earl of Bedford, Thurketil, offered his submission to Edward. In the following year Edward advanced to Bedford and took the town, apparently because there had been a revolt against him. Meantime, Ethelfleda had penetrated as far as Derby, which she took by storm.

And now Edward went on a further offensive against the Danes. He first occupied the town of Towcester which, being on Watling Street, was a frontier-post between his own territory and the Danes of Northampton. From there he advanced to a place called in *The Chronicle* 'Wigingamere' and fortified it. Alarmed by this, the Danes of Northampton attacked Towcester but failed to take it, owing to a stout resistance by Edward's men. Instead of persisting, their natural preference for plundering took over, and they went off raiding to the south, where they collected much loot 'betwixt Burnhamwood and Aylesbury'. About the same time another Danish army, from East Anglia and the Fen district, made an attempt to recapture Bedford. With this object in view they advanced their base from Huntingdon to Tempsford, about six miles north-east of Bedford, and built there a new fortress. From there they launched attacks on Bedford but were repulsed.

Yet another Danish army, from East Anglia and the parts of Mercia under Danish control, attempted to winkle the English out of their new fort at Wigingamere, but here again the English garrison held firm. The Danes rounded up what cattle they could find in the vicinity and went away.

That the Danes were meeting little success was partly due to the lack of co-ordination between their several armies, for there was now no unified command. And they were handicapped by their innate and almost irresistible urge to break off an attack on a fortified town, if they failed to take it by assault, and to go raiding instead. Alfred had rightly gauged the weakness of the enemy when he had conceived the idea of a network of fortified strongpoints. In the meantime, the English were fighting well; the garrisons knew just why they had been placed in the forts and, moreover, they were winning the war and knew it.

The forts along the Danish frontier having held out, Edward now launched a counter-stroke. While Ethelfleda was dealing with Derby and so holding down a Danish army there, Edward struck at Tempsford. After a fierce battle the English broke into the town and most of the Danes were slain, including the Danish king of East Anglia. A second prong of the attack on the East Anglian Danes invaded Essex and took the town of Colchester, also after a hotly contested battle. The English did not fortify it, however, preferring to rely on their fortifications at Maldon and Witham. A little later in the summer the East Anglian Danes staged their own counter-attack and besieged Maldon, assisted by a considerable pirate fleet (for Maldon is at the mouth of the Blackwater River). Again Edward was prepared and sent a relief force which chased the Danes away. They were now being out-manoeuvred at every turn.

In autumn Edward again took the offensive, himself leading the army in the field. He advanced from London up Watling Street to the point where the old Roman road crosses the Ouse, and there he made his head-quarters, while a detachment of the army moved on to Towcester to improve its defences with a stone wall. At the sight of this formidable force, the Danes of Northampton gave up the struggle. Under their leader, Earl Thurferth, they sent a peace delegation and 'sought him [Edward] for their lord and protector'.

Edward was well pleased and allowed the divisions of his army who had put in their period of service to go home. When the relief divisions arrived he marched them eastwards to Huntingdon, the former base of the East Anglian Danes, which he took, apparently without a fight. While Huntingdon was being rebuilt and fortified, Edward sent another contingent to do the same at Colchester: East Anglia was being ringed with his forts. The Danes caved in:

And all the Army in East Anglia swore union with him; that they would all that he would, and would protect all that he protected, either by sea or land. And the Army that belonged to Cambridge chose him separately for their lord and protector.

Early in 918 Ethelfleda took another major Danish stronghold, Leicester, apparently without a battle, 'and the greater part of the army that belonged thereto submitted to her', whereupon the Danish authorities at York sent a delegation to her, offering an alliance. They probably needed assistance against Norse raiders from Ireland, who were at that time becoming a considerable nuisance. Unfortunately, the opportunity was missed through the death of the formidable Lady of the Mercians. This happened on 12 June at Tamworth.

Edward was then at Stamford, far inside the former Danish territory, where he was constructing a strong fort south of the river Welland. In order to forestall any possible trouble over the succession, he hastened with part of his army to Tamworth, where the Mercians readily accepted him as their king. It seems, however, that they desired one of their own people to act as regent and Ethelfleda's daughter, Elfwina, exercised some sort of control until the followng winter when she was 'deprived of all authority over the Mercians and led into Wessex'. Perhaps Edward heard of intrigues going on; we cannot know.

The Mercian business settled, and Edward having also received the homage of three kings of North Wales, he returned to the Danelaw. Nottingham was next on the list for annexation, and it seems to have surrendered without a fight. Edward repaired its fortifications and had it 'manned both with English and with Danes'. Apparently the Danes were becoming willing to serve under his banner. In the next year we find him at Thelwall, a fortified borough on the south side of the Mersey near Warrington. While it was being repaired, he sent a detachment of his army across the Northumbrian border to Manchester, 'to repair and man it'. Then, in 923, he returned to Nottingham and built there a bridge across the river Trent, with a fort on the southern side to match the one already established on the northern. He also built another stronghold at Bakewell, in the Peak District of Derbyshire.

Edward was now beyond all argument the most powerful ruler in

Britain. Within 20 years he had pushed his frontier from the Thames to the Humber, and his army, flushed with success, was prepared to follow him anywhere. North of his border were three kingdoms who needed such an ally. English Northumbria—comprising Durham, Northumberland and the eastern Lowlands of Scotland—was isolated and in the midst of potential foes; it needed a protector. The Scottish kingdom of Strathclyde had been recently filching territory from its neighbours and needed an ally in case of attempted retribution. At York a Viking newcomer, Ragnald, had established a kingdom and needed a period of peace to consolidate it. The Scottish kingdom, too, needed an ally against attacks by Ragnald's compatriots in Ireland. So, in this climactic year, all of them sent delegations offering submission in return for Edward's protection. They all, records *The Chronicle* triumphantly, 'chose him as father and lord'.

The recognition of Edward's overlordship was a temporary phenomenon. Doubtless each and every one of them was prepared to renounce it when it suited him, but it provided a remarkable climax to the career of a man who could remember being a hunted fugitive in Athelney. The euphoria had not had time to disperse when the great king died, at Farndon-on-Dee, on 17 July 924.

We know little about Edward's character. Few anecdotes have attached to him, as they did to his much-loved father. We visualise him, perhaps wrongly, as a stern man, feared and respected rather than loved. Like his father, he was exceptionally patient and tenacious. As a military commander, he was outstanding: his planning was meticulous, his handling of armies masterly; he would wait until he was ready and then strike with lightning force.

Bishop Asser, setting down the life of his patron Alfred, relates one story concerning the youth of Edward. When riding one day in the country he dismounted outside the hut of a shepherd and was captivated by the beauty of the shepherd's daughter, Egwina. This girl, said Asser, had already been forewarned in a vision of her high destiny. She became the mother of the future king Athelstan, and of a daughter. There is no record of Edward having married her, but she evidently lived at court and was accepted by the family, for young Athelstan seems to have been Alfred's favourite grandson. He gave the handsome boy 'a mantle of purple, a girdle set with precious stones, and a Saxon sword in a gold scabbard'. In addition, Edward had two recognised wives, by whom he had at least 12 children. One senses that he made his own rules in such matters. And he was an impetuous man. When he wanted anything he took it, as when he seized the kingdom of Mercia and sent his niece Elfwina in exile back to Wessex.

On the other hand, although he himself had no inclination for scholarship, he appreciated the need for it. His father's measures for the education of the nobility would doubtless have impressed him, though he seems to have regarded the study of books as a feminine rather than a masculine accomplishment. William of Malmesbury tells us,

He brought up his daughters in such wise that in childhood they gave their whole attention to literature, and afterwards employed themselves in the labours of the distaff and the needle. . . . His sons were so educated that afterwards they might succeed to govern the state, not like rustics but philosophers.

In short, he followed his father's precepts in this as in military matters. Being so preoccupied with his herculean task, he tended to be neglectful of the Church, and evidently was not nearly as devout as Alfred. In fact, at one stage Pope Formosus 'sent letters to England whereby he denounced excommunication and malediction to King Edward and all his subjects . . . because for seven whole years the entire district of the West Saxons had been destitute of bishops.' When the matter was brought to his attention, however, Edward soon set about rectifying the deficiency.

His daughters married into royal families in Europe, though one was given in marriage to the king of the Northumbrians, and several became nuns. His second son, Ethelward, 'deeply versed in literature and much resembling his grandfather Alfred in features and disposition', died soon after Edward. By his third wife, Edgiva, he had two sons, Edmund and Edred, both of whom reigned after Athelstan.

And that is about all the chroniclers tell us about Edward. His epitaph must be that he built worthily and efficiently on the foundations laid by his father.

X

𝔄𝔱𝔥𝔢𝔩𝔰𝔱𝔞𝔫

As a boy, Athelstan was brought up in the court of Mercia with Ethelred and Ethelfleda, and not in his father's household in Wessex. One suspects that Edward never did marry Athelstan's mother, Egwina, and that her children were not very welcome in a household under the control of one of his official wives. For all that, the boy was accepted as a legitimate member of the family. A handsome, graceful, flaxen-haired lad, he was the favourite of his grandfather Alfred, who, as recounted on page 107, gave him lavish presents which, in the eyes of some chroniclers, were tantamount to making him heir apparent. And William of Malmesbury says that Edward in his will named Athelstan as his successor.

It was, indeed, logical that Athelstan should be the next king, for he was then a man in the prime of life, thirty years old, and trained in the hard school of warfare in which his father and his aunt Ethelfleda excelled. By his second (or third, according to whether Egwina is reckoned a wife or not) wife Edward had two sons, Edmund and Edred, who were, however, infants at the time of their father's death. Another son, Ethelward, who might have had a claim on the grounds that his mother had been married to Edward (assuming that Egwina had not been), died a few days after his father. William of Malmesbury refers to another claimant, Elfred, of whom Athelstan said in a charter many years later,

He was the jealous rival both of my happiness and life and consented to the wickedness of my enemies who, on my father's decease, had not God in his mercy delivered me, wished to put out my eyes in the city of Winchester. Wherefore, on the discovery of their infernal contrivances, he was sent to the Church of Rome to defend himself by oath before Pope John. This he did at the altar of St. Peter; but at the very instant he had sworn, he fell down before it and was carried by his servants to the English School, where he died the third night after.

There was also some mystery about the fate of another of Athelstan's half-brothers, Edwin who, according to a gossipy tale related by William of Malmesbury, was, as a punishment for being concerned in some conspiracy, placed in a leaky boat without oars and pushed out to sea to drown. A much earlier record, preserved in Flanders, says simply that Edwin was drowned at sea in an unsettled period. Whatever the truth of the matter, it seems that Athelstan's succession was not entirely uncontested. It is significant that he was first elected King of Mercia by the Mercian Witan. With the Danes still restless and having been kept under control only by Edward's strong hand, the Wessex Witan doubtless deemed it best to preserve the unity between the two kingdoms and to accept Athelstan as *their* ruler as well. But there was evidently a faction based on Winchester, the chief town of Wessex, which thought otherwise.

Once safely installed in office, Athelstan proved as capable as his father and grandfather. In his reign England rose to one of its highest peaks of prosperity and prestige. He was not only recognised as king and/or overlord of the whole of Britain but also by a series of diplomatic marriages of his sisters sealed pacts of friendship with the leading royal houses of Europe.

Investigating his status as a warrior king, however, we find him first engaged in military action in 927, three years after his accession, though there may have been unrecorded, internecine troubles during those three years. Although Edward died in July 924, it was not until September 925 that Athelstan was crowned king. Significantly the place chosen for the coronation ceremony was Kingston-on-Thames, conveniently near the border between Mercia and Wessex.

In York reigned an independent king, Sihtric, who was a cousin of the Ragnald, first Norse king of York, mentioned in the previous chapter. Soon after Athelstan's coronation this Viking monarch proposed an alliance with him: the two kings met at Tamworth, and Athelstan gave Sihtric one of his sisters in marriage. The peaceful intentions of this act were soon shattered. Only about six months later Sihtric died, and the throne was claimed by Olaf, his young son by a former wife. Olaf was brought over to Northumbria by his uncle Guthfrith, king of the Norsemen in Dublin, with an army to support him. Athelstan, though, revealed himself to be a man of action equal to his father and grandfather. Within a few weeks he had chased the army, with Guthfrith and Olaf, out of Northumbria. They retreated in such haste that Guthfrith could not get back to Ireland but took refuge with the king of the Scots, whereupon Athelstan summoned all the northern kings to meet him. The convention took place at Eamont, near Penrith, on 12 July 927, and it says much for

Athelstan's already high reputation that the kings thought it best to come. There were the kings of Scotland and Strathclyde and the Anglian king of Bernicia (the part of Northumbria north of Yorkshire), and they all swore allegiance to Athelstan. Two Welsh kings, according to *The Anglo-Saxon Chronicle*, were also present and did homage. They all promised to renounce idolatry in their kingdoms, a measure directed against the still-heathen Norsemen who were now settling in the northern and western parts of Britain. And the king of the Scots undertook to surrender the fugitive Guthfrith to Athelstan.

Guthfrith escaped while actually on his way to Eamont and, collecting a body of malcontents, rode over to York and started the war all over again. He had no better success this time. The efficient Athelstan dealt with him so effectively that, after enduring many hardships as a refugee, he was glad to surrender on his own account, and Athelstan packed him off back to Dublin. It is recorded that the citizens of York, in the true spirit of those independent burghers of the boroughs established under Edward, hurled defiance at Guthfrith when he appeared at their gates and fought hard to deny him admission. It was another triumphant vindication of the policy of Alfred and Edward in planning these boroughs, concerning which William of Malmesbury records,

He (Edward) repaired many ancient cities and built new ones in places calculated for his purpose, and filled them with a military force, to protect the inhabitants and repel the enemy. Nor was his design unsuccessful; for the inhabitants became so extremely valorous in these contests that, if they heard of any enemy approaching, they rushed out to give them battle, even without consulting the king or his generals, and constantly surpassed them both in number and in warlike skill. Thus the enemy became an object of contempt to the soldiery. . . .

The North now pacified, Athelstan turned his attention to Wales. He summoned the Welsh princes to meet him at Hereford, and again they seem to have obeyed without demur. A frontier between England and the Welsh kingdoms was agreed, and an annual tribute (of enormous dimensions, including 300 pounds of silver, 20 pounds of gold and 25,000 oxen,) to be paid by the Welsh fixed. During Athelstan's reign the Welsh princes were frequent visitors at the English court, and English influence became strong, as evinced by the laws codified by one of them, Hywel Dda, king of Dyfed.

Next on the list was Cornwall, which had apparently been causing trouble. The records seem to suggest a large-scale uprising in the South-west, extending as far as and including Exeter. Again Athelstan was swift and decisive. Defeating the Cornish, he expelled all Britons from Exeter and fixed the boundary of Cornwall on the river Tamar. The city of Exeter 'he fortified with towers and surrounded with a wall of squared stone.' Thereafter, says William of Malmesbury, the city prospered. 'Every kind of merchandise,' he records,

is there so abundant that nothing is wanting which can conduce to human comfort, . . . though the barren and unfruitful soil can scarcely produce indifferent oats and frequently only the empty husk without the grain. . . .

Anyone who is familar with the rich red soils around Exeter will find that last statement hard to believe.

Peace now lasted until 934, when Scotland grew restive. Determined to teach the Scots once and for all who was in control, Athelstan summoned his provincial commanders from every quarter, including Danes from East Anglia and Welsh princes from Wales, and prepared a formidable army. They assembled at Winchester on 28 May and were at Nottingham on 7 June. From thence they moved into Scotland, accompanied by a large fleet sailing along the east coast. The army marched as far north as Kincardineshire, plundering and ravaging, while the fleet penetrated to Caithness. The Scots did not offer battle.

It was this expedition which led, three years later, to reprisals which culminated in the Battle of Brunanburh, celebrated in song and legend for many subsequent centuries. Even *The Anglo-Saxon Chronicle* bursts into heroic verse when recording the events of that year:

> Five kings lay on the field of battle,
> In bloom of youth, pierced with swords.
> So seven eke of the earls of Anlaf;
> And of the ships' crews un-numbered crowds.
> There was dispersed the little band
> Of hardy Scots, the dread of northern hordes;
> Urged to the noisy deep by unrelenting fate. . . .
> The Northmen sailed in the nailed ships,
> A dreary remnant on the roaring sea;
> Over deep water, Dublin they sought,
> And Ireland's shores in deep disgrace. . . .

Just where the battle was fought no-one knows, but it was a mighty army that invaded England. Olaf of York, who had escaped to Dublin early in Athelstan's reign, had become accepted leader of all the Norsemen in Ireland and led the expedition. He sailed in a great fleet and collected the forces of his allies, the kings of Scotland and Strathclyde. William of Malmesbury says that Athelstan intentionally retreated before the invasion, which penetrated 'far into England'. Concerning the battle, a story is told which reminds us of Alfred entering into the camp of the Danes in the

disguise of a minstrel. Anlaf, son of Sihtric, one of the Norse heroes
mentioned in the poem quoted above, did just that. Equipped with a
harp and a repertory of old martial songs, he penetrated into Athelstan's
camp on the night before the battle and, in the intervals between entertaining the English leaders at supper, took note of the disposition of
their forces. The king, pleased with his singing, gave him a purse and
dismissed him.

The highborn Anlaf, regarding it as beneath his dignity to accept
payment for minstrelsy, buried the purse in a quiet corner, when he
thought no-one was looking. Unfortunately for him, one of the king's
servants had seen him and reported the action to Athelstan. The informer
also gave the king some good advice. It was that the king should move his
tents, which would certainly be the target for the enemy in the approaching
conflict. Athelstan considered this excellent advice and followed it.
Later in the night the Bishop of Sherborne, arriving in the camp with a
contingent of followers, saw the vacant site on level ground and proceeded
to pitch his tents there. Before morning, the enemy attacked. They made
straight for the spot where Anlaf had reported that the king was encamped, and the unlucky Bishop and his bodgyuard were annihilated.
This misdirection of effort, however, gave the king a chance to rally and
attack the enemy from the flank. The battle raged all day, but at the end
the English were wholly victorious. As the poem exultantly says, five
kings and seven earls lay dead,

> No slaughter yet was greater made
> E'er in this island, of people slain,
> Before this same, with the edge of the sword.

Constantine, king of the Scots, was one of the casualties.

As for the English, the battle of Brunanburh marked a tremendous
step forward in the union of the island races. Here, for the first time, was a
tremendous victory in which West Saxons, Mercians, Danes from the
eastern counties and Welsh from the west all shared. It gave them an
event which was common heritage, celebrated in popular heroic verse.

From that time no-one dared challenge Athelstan: he enjoyed the
final two years of his reign in a haze of glory. From Land's End to the
Firth of Forth England was firmly under his control and apparently
perfectly content with the situation. Beyond the frontiers Wales, Scotland,
Strathclyde and even Ireland accepted his domination with acquiesence,
being in no condition to do otherwise.

Overseas he was regarded as one of the leading monarchs of Europe.
He married one of his sisters to Hugh, duke of the Franks, who was the

effective ruler of Frankland. Henry the Fowler, the German king who was welding together the scattered fragments of the eastern half of Charlemagne's empire, sent an embassy to ask for another of Athelstan's sisters for his son Otto. Athelstan obligingly sent two of them to Otto from which to choose. The young man selected Edith, the elder; and the surplus younger sister was married off to 'a certain duke, near the Alps', probably Conrad of Burgundy. A third sister was given to Louis, prince of Aquitaine. Athelstan's family connections with the ruling-houses of Europe were hence unsurpassed. His alliances led to a couple of undistinguished adventures on the Continent. When Louis d'Outremer became king of the Franks, by permission of Hugh Capet, Athelstan dispatched a fleet to help repel a German invasion. And Englishmen apparently helped Alan, ruler of Britanny, to recover a nucleus of his domain from invading Norsemen. The part the English played was a minor one, in both instances, but never before had they been strong enough to become involved in continental affairs.

Athelstan was even approached by Harold Fairhair, first king of a united Norway, with a mission of friendship and it is said that Haakon, Harold's son was brought up in Athelstan's household. The gift Harold sent with the embassy was, according to William of Malmesbury, 'a ship with a golden beak and purple sail, furnished within with a compacted fence of gilded shields'. Henry the Fowler's presents to Athelstan included

perfumes such as never had been seen in England before; jewels, but more especially emeralds . . . many fleet horses with their trappings, an alabaster vase, exquisitely chased, the sword of Constantine the Great, the spear of Charles the Great

and numerous other treasures as well as an impressive collection of sacred relics, which Athelstan had a passion for collecting.

The English court continued to be peripatetic, moving from place to place in accordance with local food-supplies. Of the list of places where Athelstan is known to have held court, most are in Wessex. His court, and the national council or Witan, had expanded considerably from the small band of intimates that served Alfred, though that was inevitable with the expansion of the realm. Alfred's insistence on a form of universal education had borne fruit to the extent that literacy was now quite common in England. It resulted in a spate of charters, most of them confirming royal grants of land. Many survive and show by their language, which tends to be florid and pretentious rather than precise, that the new literary élite were not necessarily literary stylists.

However, they do throw much valuable light on the domestic scene in Anglo-Saxon England in the tenth century.

Athelstan is said to have been of medium height, thin and—according to William of Malmesbury who claimed to have seen his remains—'his hair flaxen, beautifully wreathed with gold threads'. He was as devout as his grandfather Alfred and generous with his donations, especially to religious foundations, 'To the nobility rather reserved; to the lower classes, he was kind and condescending'. His generosity to the Church ensured that he received a good obituary. He died in the year 939, aged about 44. His reign had thus lasted only 15 years. The cause of his death is not known, but it seems that the fatal family weakness, perhaps connected with Alfred's mysterious malady, was making its existence felt. Future generations looked back on Athelstan's reign as a Golden Age.

XI

Edmund and Edred

If Egbert's dynasty was beginning to reveal the unfortunate hereditary weakness which cut short the careers of member after member, it had a compensatory asset which was serving them well—they had an extraordinary family solidarity. One has only to look at the contemporary scene on the Continent, where Charlemagne's great empire had dissolved in feuds and fratricidal wars, to appreciate how remarkable was the harmony which prevailed, with a few exceptions, in the royal house of Wessex. When eventually it did crack, with disastrous results for England, the split was introduced from outside, by a selfish and ruthless queen.

The spectacle of brother peaceably succeeding brother, for which the sons of Ethelwulf created a precedent, was now to be repeated by the sons of Edward. For the smoothness with which the exercise was completed some of the credit must undoubtedly go to the Witan or Council, which had demonstrated time and again their authority to elect to the throne whichever member of the royal family was most eminently suitable for the job. Nevertheless, it is also true that the other members of the family accepted the decision with good grace if, indeed, they did not help in making it, and thereafter gave their loyal support to the successful candidate.

This unusual lack of jealousy and resentment served the country extremely well in that reigning monarchs were not averse from giving men, who in less closely-knit families would have had to be regarded as potential rivals or usurpers, extensive responsibility, even to the extent of allowing them to command armies. Thus King Ethelred had had no hesitation in co-operating with Alfred, readily giving Alfred the position of second-in-command, while Alfred in his turn had permitted Edward to command strong armies in his lifetime; Edward sent Athelstan to learn the art of war under his brother-in-law, Ethelred, and his sister, Ethelfleda. And then Athelstan had associated with himself, in the leadership of the English armies, his half-brother Edmund.

Edmund, the son of Edward's third wife, Edgiva, was only a small boy, of not more than three, when Edward died. Athelstan could have seen in him a future rival, especially if legitimacy was reckoned an important factor, for while we do not know whether Athelstan's mother was married to Edward, Edmund's certainly was. Yet Athelstan had unhesitatingly accepted the care of Edmund and his younger brother Edred, allowing them to live with his household and seeing that they were properly educated. At the Battle of Brunanburh, when Edmund was about sixteen, Athelstan allowed the promising lad to share the command with him. The two fought together in the battle and were together commemorated in the songs that circulated throughout Britain:

> Here Athelstan king, of earls the lord,
> Rewarder of heroes, and his brother eke,
> Edmund atheling, elder of ancient race,
> Slew in the fight with the edge of their swords,
> The foe at Brunanburh. . . .

So, having shared in Athelstan's glory, on his death Edmund, then aged eighteen, was accepted his successor. From the beginning he inherited trouble. As in Athelstan's time, it came in the north. In the last few years of Edward's reign a Viking, Ragnald, had become the first Norse king at York. His cousin Sihtric, after a short reign, was succeeded by his son Olaf who, as has been revealed, brought over an army of Norwegians from Dublin and was chased away by Athelstan. The invasion which culminated in the battle of Brunanburh was instigated by the Irish Norse.

Licking their wounds after their overwhelming defeat, the Norsemen in Ireland naturally saw the death of their conqueror and the accession of an eighteen-year-old lad as a new opportunity. Athelstan died at the end of October. Before the end of December the Irish Norse, led by King Olaf Guthfrithson, were back in York, and a month or so later Olaf led a devastating raid into the heart of the Midlands. Checked at Northampton, he veered westwards across Mercia, sacking the old royal burgh of Tamworth and destroying and plundering everywhere.

Edmund quickly collected an army and marched to meet the invaders. He caught up with them at Leicester as they were returning home with their spoils, and a tremendous battle seemed imminent. But the Church intervened to prevent the threatened bloodshed. The archbishops of Canterbury and York met and between them they arranged a peace treaty which they were able to persuade the rival kings to accept. Doubtless they had little trouble with Olaf, for the terms were heavily weighted in his favour. The whole of the Danelaw, from Watling Street to the Northumbrian border (roughly the present southern border of Yorkshire), was ceded to him. Edmund must have needed more persuasion, but perhaps his advisers considered the odds against him and urged him to wait until he was firmly established on his throne and had gathered more strength. That, at any rate, was what Edmund did. The peace of Leicester was formulated in 940. It lasted for two years. In 942 Edmund launched an attack against the Norsemen of York and won back all the surrendered territories.

Describing the campaign, *The Anglo-Saxon Chronicle* again bursts into verse, in the course of which it expresses sentiments that would have seemed incredible to earlier generations:

> In thraldom long to Northern Danes
> They bowed through need and dragged the chains
> Of heathen men; till, to his glory,
> Great Edward's heir, Edmund the king,
> Refuge of warriors, their fetters broke.

In other words, the Danes of the Danelaw regarded the Norsemen of York and Ireland as oppressors, much preferring to be ruled by English kings. As if to emphasise his meaning, the chronicler specifically lists the Five Boroughs of the Danes—Leicester, Lincoln, Nottingham, Stamford and Derby. The poem underlines the fact, often forgotten, that the Danes and Norwegians were at this stage bitter enemies, fighting each other whenever they had an opportunity. The Danes settled in eastern England evidently felt that they had more in common with the English than with these plundering Norsemen. Besides, they had just enjoyed 15 years of peace under the tolerant rule of Athelstan, who seems to have allowed them a good measure of self-government and to have been on good terms with Danish earls, who frequented his court. They were pleased to see Edmund back.

A word here about events at York. Returning from Leicester, Olaf turned northwards and invaded the still independent English kingdom of Northumbria, reaching from the Tees to the Forth. Having spread devastation throughout the entire country he died. His successor was another Olaf, Olaf Sihtricson (the son of that Sihtric who had been the second king of York). It was he who was opposed to Edmund when the latter began the campaign which regained the Danelaw. Probably as a result of his failure in this war, the Norse Northumbrians expelled him and put a brother of Olaf Guthfrithson, another Ragnald, in his place.

Each of these two claimants to the throne at York now sought Edmund's aid. Each visited him and accepted baptism into the Christian faith, evidently as a necessary condition of his assistance. Then they went back to York and prepared to fight it out. But in 944 Edmund, exasperated by their intrigues, led an army to York and chased them both away. It seems that one or the other of them escaped to the Celtic kingdom of Strathclyde and carried on subversion from there, for in the following year, 946, Edmund embarked on a major invasion of Strathclyde. Both *The Anglo-Saxon Chronicle* and *The Annals of the Britons* briefly recall the event, the former stating that 'this year King Edmund overran all Cumberland', the latter that 'Strat Clud was devastated by the Saxons'. It is also recorded that Edmund had made an alliance with the new king of Scotland, Malcolm, and when his conquest of Strathclyde was completed, 'let it all to Malcolm, on the condition that he became his ally both by sea and by land'.

Edmund, now twenty-four, seemed on the threshold of a career that would equal if not surpass that of Athelstan. He had proved himself both in battle and in diplomacy. The entire island of Great Britain was either under his direct control or in the hands of friendly monarchs, notably the king of the Scots. In the last few months of his reign he was preparing to exert his influence in foreign affairs, sending an embassy to Frankland to support Louis d'Outremer in his attempts to regain his kingdom.

Then occurred a tragedy which robbed England of a potentially great king. On the feast of St. Augustine, in May, when the king and his court were feasting at Pucklechurch, Gloucestershire, Edmund suddenly caught sight of a robber whom he had banished for his crimes some six years previously. Here was this man, Leofa, sitting feasting at his table. Filled with indignation, the king jumped up from his seat and dashing down the hall, seized Leofa by the hair and dragged him to the floor. Instinctively, Leofa pulled out a dagger and stabbed his assailant to the heart. The startled guests and the king's attendants rushed at him and 'tore him limb from limb, though he wounded some of them ere they could accomplish their purpose'. But Edmund was dead probably before he was.

He was unfeignedly mourned throughout England, as well he might be, and was buried with great pomp in Glastonbury Abbey. He left two infant sons, Edwy and Edgar, but as they were both so young the king's brother, Edred, was elected to succeed him.

Edred, the third of Edward's sons to occupy the English throne, carried on the family tradition worthily. Primarily king of Wessex, he was accepted also by the Mercians, the Danes of the Danelaw and, at first, by the Northumbrians. At a place which *The Chronicle* calls 'Tadden's-cliff', where afterwards Pontefract Castle was raised, Edred met and received the allegiance of the authorities of the North, including Archbishop Wulfstan of York, who had been one of the prime architects of the treaty of Leicester. Throughout his career Wulfstan seems to have been interested more in the independence of the North than in collaboration with the south, as events were about to demonstrate.

As already noted, during Athelstan's reign Harold Fairhair succeeded in welding together the squabbling clans of Norway into a united kingdom. On his death he was succeeded by one of his sons, Eric, nicknamed 'Bloodaxe'. Eric proved so tyrannical, amply earning his *sobriquet*, that the Norwegians deposed him, electing in his place his more civilised half-brother Haakon, who had been brought up at Athelstan's court. Whereupon Eric, collecting a band of like-minded comrades, acquired a fleet of ships and departed over the western sea to seek his fortune in another land. After several raids here and there he arrived in Northumbria, where he was welcomed by the Norse residents and established himself as king at York. The old pattern of events was repeating itself.

Edred accepted the challenge in the traditional manner, marching north with a formidable army and proceeding to ravage Norse Northumbria. He fought no major battle until returning south, when he was caught with part of his army on the wrong side of the river Aire at Castleford. It seems that Edred had gone on towards York and that in a surprise attack the Norsemen overwhelmed the rearguard. *The Chronicle* records that Edred was so angry that he wanted to return straight away to the north of Yorkshire 'and lay waste the land withal'. But when the Northumbrian Council understood what was threatened, and knowing that Edred was quite capable of carrying out his threat 'they abandoned Eric'.

The next year Olaf Sihttricson appears on the scene again, apparently returning from Dublin. This was either by arrangement or with the connivance of Edred, for the latter was apparently content to let him rule in York for three years. Then, in 952, Eric came back again, and the unlucky Olaf, deposed for the second time, returned sadly to Dublin. The reign of Eric Bloodaxe at York seems to have endured no more than two years, but an extant poem depicts him ruling there in high state, feasting in his great hall and intriguing against his old enemies in Norway. English Northumbria, however, appears to have adhered to Edred, for *The Chronicle* states that Archbishop Wulfstan, whom the English held largely to blame for these frequent defections of York, was chained in prison at Jedburgh.

In 954 Edred resumed control of Norse Northumbria. The course of events is obscure. *The Chronicle* says that 'the Northumbrians expelled Eric', and later traditions tell how, as a fugitive with a few companions, he fled over the northern moors until treacherously killed 'at Steinmore' by Earl Maccus, son of Olaf, probably Olaf Sihtricson, whom he had chased out of York. A person in some way involved in his betrayal was Earl

Oswulf, who ruled whatever remained of English Northumbria, north of the Tees, throughout the years of the Norse regime in York. He probably acknowledged some sort of allegiance to Edred, for after Eric's death Edred gave him the whole of southern Northumbria (Yorkshire) as well, though he never aspired to be more than an earl.

The North thus pacified, King Edred released Archbishop Wulfstan from jail and restored him to a bishopric, though this time to the see of Dorchester-on-Thames, well away from his own country and safe in loyal Wessex, where he could be watched. Edred's reign was drawing to a close, as he probably realised. For years he had been more or less an invalid. Though as successful a warrior as his father and brothers he, like his grandfather Alfred, had to battle all the time with a physical handicap. William of Malmesbury, quoting more ancient documents, says that he was

constantly oppressed by sickness, and of so weak a digestion as to be unable to swallow more than the juices of the food he had masticated, to the great annoyance of his guests.

Yet he personally led his armies and was as tough as the times demanded for, as William of Malmesbury states,

he nearly exterminated the Northumbrians and the Scots, laying waste the whole province with sword and famine, because, having with little difficulty compelled them to swear fidelity to him, they broke their oath and made Eric their king.

In this campaign he did nothing to prevent his troops from setting fire to the old minster church at Ripon, founded by St. Wilfrid, and *The Chronicle* further records that in 954 'the king ordered a great slaughter to be made in the town of Thetford, in revenge of the abbot, whom they had formerly slain.' Edred was evidently not a man to be trifled with. A military leader who could so speedily deal with a Norse hero like Eric Bloodaxe must have been a formidable character.

His monastic biographers, however, record another side of his personality, as summarised by William of Malmesbury, who writes that he devoted his life to God, 'endured with patience his frequent bodily pains, prolonged his prayers and made his palace altogether the school of virtue.' He died, says William, 'accompanied with the utmost grief of men but joy of angels'.

Edred reigned for nine or ten years and was only in his middle thirties when he died. The fatal physical weakness inherent in the family of Egbert was continuing to take its toll of these gifted men, nor was its menace abated in the next generation, for of Edred's two nephews, who succeeded him, Edwy died in his 'teens and Edgar was not more than thirty-two.

Strictly speaking, Edred was the last of the series of warrior kings of the Wessex dynasty, though this was largely because they had done their work so well that the next two monarchs of the line, Edwy and Edgar, had no need to demonstrate their military prowess. Edgar indeed enjoyed all the prestige of a successful conqueror without having to fight for it. For over 100 years successive generations of the royal family of Wessex had fought to a standstill the most ferocious menace the Christian West had ever known. While far more renowned kingdoms and empires on the Continent fell and dissolved in chaos, the indomitable West Saxons stood firm, forced the enemy back step by slow step and eventually moulded both their shattered people and such of their foes who were prepared to settle down into the beginnings of a unified state. No other nation can approach their record. The names of these Warrior Kings are worthy to be inscribed in letters of gold, in the most sacred shrine of the nation:

EGBERT

ETHELWULF

ETHELBALD

ETHELBERT

ETHELRED

ALFRED

EDWARD

ATHELSTAN

EDMUND

EDRED

Nor was the last of the line any less illustrious than the first.

XII

Edwy and Edgar

The term 'the last of the line' with which the last chapter concluded is true only as regards the 'warrior' aspect of our title. The line of kings of the royal house of Wessex continued unbroken. On the death of Edred, who had no children, the claims of the sons of his brother Edmund had natural priority. Both were still boys, though not too young to be considered for kingship. Edwy, the elder, was fourteen or fifteen; Edgar twelve. Under such circumstances the position of the king's council is naturally enhanced, and the West Saxon kings were traditionally well served in this respect. One of Edred's close friends was Dunstan, who achieved a position of dominance in the reign of Edgar and was subsequently canonised. Other powerful notables whose names we know were Alderman Byrhtnoth of Essex, Alderman Elfhere of Mercia, Alderman Elfheah of Hampshire and Alderman Ethelwold of East Anglia.

Edwy, who reigned for only four years, was badly treated by medieval historians. He deliberately antagonised Dunstan and, in fact, stripped him of his possessions and offices and drove him into exile. Monastic chroniclers of future ages, to whom Dunstan was a saint and on whom we rely for most of our information of the period, naturally regarded this as illustrative of Edwy's depravity and made the most of it. The root of the quarrel, as recounted by most of the writers who deal with Edwy's reign, lay in an incident on the day that Edwy was consecrated king. When all the dignitaries of the kingdom were assembled and, says William of Malmesbury, 'deliberating on affairs of importance and essential to the state', it was noticed that Edwy had left the meeting. Dunstan and another bishop who were sent to discover where he had got to, found him enjoying the company of a noble lady and her daughter. Dunstan,

regardless of the royal indignation, violently dragged the lascivious boy from the chamber and . . . compelling him to repudiate the strumpet, made him his enemy for ever.

123

The report is hardly fair, for Edwy later married the younger of the two ladies, a development which her mother was doubtless encouraging when interrupted by Dunstan. Queen Elgifu was, in her widowhood, regarded as among 'the most illustrious of women', and Edwy himself, in his short reign, continued to make grants to churches and other religious establishments on much the same scale as his predecessors. It was just unfortunate for his posthumous reputation that he detested Dunstan, and in this he was undoubtedly influenced by his mother-in-law. Probably his dislike had reasonable grounds, for Dunstan was a strong man but not an especially comfortable character to live with, while he was pretty high-handed in his dealing with women, whom he tended to regard as instruments of the devil.

Whether or not Dunstan had anything to do with it, in 975, two years after he had been chosen as king, Edwy was rejected by the councils of Mercia and probably Northumbria in favour of his brother Edgar. Then for two years Edwy continued to reign in Wessex, while Edgar was king in the Midlands and the North. In 959 Edwy, still not twenty, died, whether from hereditary weakness or some other cause is not known. Upon which Edgar, now sixteen, was acknowledged as king by the whole nation.

Edwy, it is recorded, was a youth of remarkable beauty. His nickname (most of the Saxon kings and nobles had nicknames) was 'All-fair'. He seems to have been a headstrong and impetuous young man, though perhaps no more so than could be expected of a royal prince in those turbulent times. Though the records contain no hint of anything amiss, one wonders about his early death.

One of the first acts of Edgar was to recall the exiled Dunstan, whom he forthwith made Bishop of Worcester and later Bishop of London. Thenceforth, the reign of Edgar is equally the reign of Dunstan. Edgar was evidently a pliable character who, in most respects, did as Dunstan 'advised' and was consequently praised to high heaven by the monks who kept the records, though in personal and sexual matters he seems to have been less amenable to ecclesiastical discipline. Because of these personal aberrations his coronation at Bath in 973 was postponed until he had been on the throne for 13 years.

A word here on the career of Dunstan will not be out-of-place. Born at Baltonsborough, a village in Somerset, he was related to the royal family and nephew to Athelm, the Bishop of Bath & Wells. Nepotism was pretty prevalent in those days. Having been educated at Glastonbury Dunstan, through the influence of his uncle, obtained a post at the royal court (the king then being Athelstan) where he seemed destined for a career as a courtier or alderman. His strong character, however, attracted a good deal of opposition, which crystallised into a plot against him. Athelstan was persuaded to banish him, and, as he rode away into exile, his enemies way-laid him, rolled him in the mud and stamped on him. He managed to stag-ger to a friend's house where, while convalescing and in the lonely months which followed, he became convinced that the Church was his vocation.

When Edmund became king he sent for Dunstan, who soon rose to the position of chief adviser. Again his strong, dogmatic attitude gave rise to bitter antagonism and Edmund, like Athelstan, was persuaded to sentence him to exile. At this juncture Edmund, based on the royal estate at Cheddar, went hunting on Mendip. His horse bolted on the hill plateau and made straight for the lip of the Cheddar Gorge. Edmund, face-to-face with imminent death, repented of his treatment of Dunstan and swore to reinstate him if only he were saved. The horse swerved on the very edge of the cliff, and Edmund went back to Cheddar to tell Dunstan that instead of exile he was to receive the gift of the great estate of Glastonbury, of which he was henceforth Abbot. Dunstan continued to serve both Edmund and Edred as chief counsellor, again suffered banishment under Edwy, and resumed his position at the court of Edgar.

During all the 15 years of Edgar's reign the chronicles contain scarcely a mention of war or unrest. Apparently there was an Irish raid on West-morland in 966, and some incident in Thanet caused Edgar to send an avenging contingent of the army there in 969, but that was all. Neverthe-less, the profound peace does not mean that the enemies of England lacked the will to take up arms. The disasters that followed so soon after the death of Edgar showed that there were still many adversaries ready to exploit weakness. By inference, then, Edgar was recognised as a strong ruler—it was appreciated that he could not be challenged with impunity. He deserves a place among the Warrior Kings of Saxon England, even if he never had to fight.

William of Malmesbury recounts a story that illustrates Edgar's personal courage. The king was a very short man, less than five feet tall. 'At a certain banquet ... Kinad, king of the Scots, said in a sportive manner that it seemed extraordinary to him how so many provinces should be subject to such a sorry little fellow.' A minstrel, overhearing this, repeated it before King Edgar, with a good deal of raillery. When he had an opportunity, Edgar persuaded Kinad to accompany him to a wood, on the pretext of asking his advice, and then suddenly drew two swords, one of which he presented to Kinad, with the words,

Now, as we are alone, I shall have opportunity of proving your strength. I will now make it appear which ought deservedly to command the other; nor shall you stir a foot till you try the matter with me.

The alarmed king of the Scots, seeing nothing but disaster ahead even if he happened to win the contest, fell down at Edgar's feet and begged pardon, explaining that it had all been a joke. Edgar accepted the explanation.

The chronicles delight in relating how Edgar, after his coronation in 973, sailed with his fleet to Chester where six kings rowed his barge on the river Dee. The list appears to include kings of Wales, Strathclyde and either a Norse or Danish king, as well as the king of the Scots. The tale is probably true, though there was probably more pageantry than compulsion about the matter, for Edgar seems to have been on excellent terms with his guests. It is also recorded that every year he sent his fleets right around the island, keeping a look-out for pirates. He himself, with his army and his court in attendance, patrolled the great Roman roads, visiting province after province and enquiring after the dispensation of justice. He evidently appreciated that the price of peace was constant vigilance.

Edgar used the peace to further the prosperity of the kingdom. He reorganised the administration of England, shaping the shires which endured for 1000 years and subdividing them into hundreds, each with its court. He revised the laws, giving extensive autonomy to the Danish districts, and enforced the observance of his statutes with rigorous severity. William of Malmesbury relates,

Edgar's laws for the punishment of offenders were horribly severe. The eyes were put out, nostrils slit, ears torn off, hands and feet cut off and, finally the scalp torn off, the miserable wretches were left exposed to birds or beasts of prey.

Horrific though such penalties were, they had the desired effect. It was said that in Edgar's day a woman with a baby could walk unharmed anywhere in his domains. We may surmise that there was little crime in Edgar's England.

Peace established, under Dunstan's guidance Edgar made it one of his chief tasks to encourage the restoration of old monasteries and the foundation of new ones. One of William of Malmesbury's complaints about King Edwy was that 'even the monstery of Malmesbury (his own domicile), which had been inhabited by monks for more than 250 years, he made a sty for secular canons'. This, said William, was typical of what was happening all over England. Edgar reversed the trend. New Benedictine houses were established and the monks naturally took the lead in improving the arts of civilisation. They introduced forgotten aspects of agriculture, such as the growing of wheat and the cultivation of vines; they practised the old arts of illuminating manuscripts and figure sculpture; they reclaimed marshland and created fish-ponds. Wealth accumulated, much of it crystallised—as before the Danish invasions—in church treasures. The golden age which had begun in the reign of Athelstan continued and expanded under the brilliant rule of Edgar. The climax of the reign was marked by Edgar's coronation at Bath in 973, a magnificent event for which Dunstan composed a programme which has been the basis of English coronations ever since.

As mentioned earlier, the reason for the delay in the coronation was Edgar's reputation as a libertine. In this respect he seems to have been not unlike his brother Edwy. One particular offence for which Dunstan imposed a long penance was the abduction of a novice nun by force. On another occasion he arrived at Andover and demanded the beautiful daughter of a local nobleman for a bed-companion. The girl's mother, shocked, substituted a servant girl, though also beautiful, when it was too dark for the king to notice the difference. In the morning the girl got up early and dressed. When Edgar asked her what was the hurry she replied, 'To perform the daily duty of my mistress'. Edgar then elicited the truth from her and considered how he should deal with the matter. Eventually he decided to regard the whole affair as a joke, or so he said:

But soon afterwards he exalted her with great honour, to be mistress of her former tyrants, little consulting how they liked it, loved her entirely nor left her bed till he took Elfrida to be his legitimate wife.

One can imagine that, with a strong king like Edgar, the rest of the court appreciated the joke at the expense of the unfortunate nobleman of Andover.

The episode of Elfrida was, however, more serious and had permanent effects on the realm. It happened that Edgar heard of the beauty of Elfrida (or Elfthryth), the daughter of Earl Ordgar of Devonshire, so he sent a trusted nobleman, Ethelwold, down to Devonshire to find out whether the reports had been exaggerated. Ethelwold not only discovered that they were not but promptly fell in love with her himself. So he went back to the king with the report that she was a typical apple-cheeked Devonshire dumpling, but that as she was so rich he would rather like to marry her himself for her inheritance. To this the king agreed, and Ethelwold and Elfrida were duly wed.

In due course, gossips carried to Edgar the rumour that he had been deceived. So, when on a hunting expedition in the south-west, he sent a message to Ethelwold that he proposed to visit his home and to enjoy his hospitality. Ethelwold, 'terrified almost to death', begged his wife to make herself as ugly and unattractive as possible for the occasion. It would have needed a very devoted wife to accede to that request, and certainly Elfrida was not such a woman. Probably she herself was hearing the story for the first time and was in no mood to protect a husband who had so deceived her and robbed her of a probable crown. When Edgar arrived she appeared dressed in her finest clothes and looking as seductive as art and her natural charms could make her. Edgar fell immediately. As soon as was convenient he invited Ethelwold to go hunting with him in Harewood Forest, in Hampshire, and there killed him with a javelin. Then he sent to Devonshire for Elfrida, whom he forthwith married.

Elfrida gave him two sons, the older of which died while still a boy, while the second, Ethelred, was about ten years old in 975, when his father died. In addition to these two, Edgar had a son Edward, and a daughter Edith, by a previous marriage to the daughter of another earl. His death, at the age of thirty-two or thereabouts, was sudden and unexpected. With it the firm government, which he had controlled with so steady a hand, collapsed.

After him, as later historians reported of Louis XIV, came the deluge.

XIII

𝔅𝔩𝔬𝔬𝔡𝔰𝔥𝔢𝔡 𝔞𝔫𝔡 𝔇𝔞𝔯𝔨𝔫𝔢𝔰𝔰

Her career as the consort of one king having ended with the death of Edgar, the ambitious and unscrupulous Elfrida now determined to be the mother of the next. Only one life stood between her son Ethelred and the throne.

Edward, Edgar's elder son by another wife, had unfortunately made himself widely unpopular, though still only a youth of about sixteen. William of Malmesbury, writing more than 100 years later and doubtless influenced by the fact that by that time Edward was regarded as a saint, says that he followed 'the footsteps of his father's piety, giving both his attention and his heart to good counsel'. Modern historians however, delving into other sources, find that Edward had a reputation for violent outbursts of rage in which he quite lost control of himself, to the alarm of his family and household. William's assessment of his character was probably coloured by the identity of the minister who provided Edward with good counsel, namely Dunstan. The controversy over the accession seems to have developed into a struggle between Dunstan and his allies and a powerful group of nobles, notably several Mercians, who preferred Ethelred. Linked with the personality clash was a strong anti-monastic sentiment. The favour that Edgar had shown to monasticism evidently bred its own reaction. It was widely felt that the monasteries had grown too rich to quickly. In such circumstances, avarice and covetousness undoubtedly played their part. Many nobles must have been tempted by the likelihood that in any general stripping of monastic assets some of the property would fall to them. Another factor was the unpopularity of Archbishop Dunstan: the hostility which that haughty prelate provoked was really something remarkable.

It is to this short reign of Edward the Martyr that the well-known anecdote of Dunstan and the conference at Calne belongs. The subject being debated was the paramount one concerning the control of the monasteries. Dunstan and his supporters took the side of the monks, those who held the opposite viewpoint maintained it, says William of Malmesbury, 'with much animosity and debate, directing the weapons of harsh reproach' against Dunstan. 'Men of every rank were earnestly defending their several sides of the question' when the floor of the upper room in which they were assembled gave way and precipitated them all into the room below. All, that is, except Dunstan, 'who alone escaped unhurt by standing on a single rafter which retained its position.' Every one of the others was either killed or badly injured. William refers to the event as 'this miracle', but for us in a less credulous age there must be at least a suspicion that it was a manufactured one.

During his reign of three-and-a-half years Edward, again according to William, 'conducted himself with becoming affection towards his infant brother and his stepmother.' William tells us nothing about fits of rage and ungovernable temper; to him Edward was virtuous, by way of contrast to the feckless Ethelred. At any rate, he was on sufficiently friendly terms to call on Elfrida at Corfe (Dorset) when tired and thirsty after a day's hunting. She received him with every token of affection but, while he was drinking from the cup she gave him, she signalled to her attendants to creep up behind him, and one of them sank a dagger into his back. At least, that is the tale William of Malmesbury tells, though the earliest records do not actually name Elfrida as the instigator of the crime. 'Dreadfully wounded,' writes William,

with all his remaining strength he clapped spurs to his horse in order to join his companions, when, one foot slipping, he was dragged by the other through the trackless paths and recesses of the wood, while the streaming blood gave evidence of his death to his followers.

Men in those violent days could tolerate violence which would shock us, but they could not stomach treachery of this order. His faults forgotten, the murdered Edward was soon regarded as a saint and martyr. There was something to be said for the attitude. Sainthood in the Dark Ages had little to do with personal morality. A king in particular was a sacred person. At the coronation ceremony the most solemn moment was not the placing of the crown on the monarch's head but the anointing. By this the king was consecrated to the service of God through service to his people. He was a priest as well as a king. The killing of a king by members of his own family was therefore a crime which filled the nation with foreboding. No good would come to a people who had slain the Lord's Anointed. The murder took place on 18 March 978 and the corpse of the king was interred in haste at Wareham, Dorset. Soon, however, it became a place of pilgrimage. Mysterious lights were seen hovering above the tomb, and lame, blind, deaf and sick folk, hastening thither, were cured of their infirmities.

Guilty consciences began to work. Alfhere, the alderman of Mercia who had been so strenuously opposed to Edward and Dunstan, 'being deeply distressed in his mind, took up the sacred corpse from its unworthy resting-place and paid it just and distinguished honours at Shaftesbury.' Elfrida attempted to stop the rot by riding in state to the tomb, but her favourite horse, though urged by whips and spurs, refused to approach it. Convinced at last that she had committed an unforgiveable crime, or perhaps attempting to convince other people that she was repentant, she retired to a nunnery at Wherwell in Harewood Forest—the nunnery that Edgar had founded in penance for his own murder of her first husband—and there spent the rest of her life mortifying the flesh by such devices as wearing hair-cloth and sleeping at nights on the ground without a pillow.

This was all very well, but the common people expected further retribution to follow. Edward had been the representative whom God had appointed to govern them, and their superstitious minds could not believe that God would allow the guilty to escape unscathed. They waited with a sense of impending doom for the blow to fall. When new calamities visited their country, they knew why. The same fatalistic conviction may have been in the mind of Ethelred and may do much to explain his vacillations and ineffectiveness. It was as though he 'knew' that whatever he did was foredoomed to failure. He was aware that he occupied a position that rightfully belonged to another man—one, moreover, who had been murdered to make room for him. It was no sort of attitude of mind in which to meet the trials that lay ahead.

Ethelred, then presumably about fourteen, was consecrated king 'on the Sunday fortnight after Easter, of the year 979, at Kingston'. Thus *The Anglo-Saxon Chronicle*, which adds,

this same year was seen a bloody welkin oft-times in the likeness of fire; and that was most apparent at midnight, and so in misty beams was shown; but when it began to dawn, then it glided away.

After such a portent no-one could be surprised when, in the following year, a new series of Danish raids began. The reason for this sudden resurgence of energy in the northern peoples was partly due to events in their homeland. An exceptionally strong king, Harold Gormsson, had succeeded in uniting all Denmark and Norway into a single kingdom and then in imposing Christianity on his subjects as the state religion. It was he who established the great Viking stronghold Jomsborg, celebrated in northern sagas, on the Oder. His ruthless actions sent many opponents and probably many adherents of the old Norse religion into exile overseas. They turned to the old northern trade of raiding and, to their delight, found in England a crop of plunder ripe for the picking. The ordeals that had been imposed on England more than 100 years earlier were to be repeated.

Blame can hardly be attached to Ethelred when things began to go wrong from the very beginning of his reign. He was, after all, only ten years old when his brother was murdered. Although he benefited, he could not have been responsible.

The year after his coronation, 980, a Danish pirate fleet crept up Southampton Water and stormed Southampton. 'Most of the population was slain or imprisoned,' says *The Anglo-Saxon Chronicle*. Another plundering band caused havoc in Thanet, while yet another slipped around to Cheshire. In the following year Danish pirates did much damage in Cornwall, Devon and Wales. In 982 three Viking ships landed at Portland and sacked it. 'The same year was London burned', says *The Chronicle*, presumably by Danes. Then came five or six years of peace when at least no major raids were recorded. By the time they were resumed in 987 Ethelred was nineteen—an age of full manhood in those days and one at which many of his illustrious predecessors on the throne of Wessex had already won renown on the battle-field and in the council chamber. We can imagine how Edward (Alfred's son), or Athelstan, or Edmund, or Edgar would have dealt with the Danish challenge.

But in every reign there *was* a challenge. Danes and disaffected Saxons tested the nerve of each new monarch, who needed to act quickly and effectively if he were to retain his throne. Fortunately, as we have seen, king after king of the House of Egbert had proved equal to the situation. Their record is indeed remarkable. Now it was to be broken. Ethelred was not a warrior king of the calibre of his ancestors, and his failure sets their successes in sharper relief. In his reign the pirates ventured, as they had so often done before, and got away with their plunder. Therefore they came again.

After the hiatus, the raids were resumed in 987, when a minor intrusion was made at Watchet. In 988 they were in Devon, defeating the local levies in a large-scale battle in which the Saxon commander was slain. In this same year the redoubtable Dunstan died, his death removing a pillar on which the weak king might have depended for support. In 991 a pirate-fleet sacked Ipswich, then sailed south along the Essex coast and anchored in the estuary of the river Blackwater. There they were brought to bay by the local English commander, Alderman Byrhtnoth, in a battle which inspired one of the finest of early English epic poems, *The Battle of Maldon*.

The course of the battle illustrates graphically both what was right and what was wrong with the English defences. The Danes were camped on Northey Island, on the south side of the Blackwater estuary, which was connected with the mainland only by a causeway which was submerged at high tide. Byrhtnoth and his army arrived on the shore opposite the island when the tide was high and took up their positions to wait either for a siege or an attempted break-out. As the tide began to ebb the Danes attacked but could do so only three abreast along the causeway, where they were held by three English stalwarts who killed them off as fast as they came. After an interlude in which the Danes came off much the worse, their leaders shouted to Byrhtnoth that he was taking an unfair advantage. 'Let us come across, so that at least we can fight on equal terms,' they taunted, and the chivalrous Byrhtnoth agreed. The Danes swarmed over, the two armies drew up in battle array, and soon they were hard at it, hewing away with battle-axe and sword. But now it seems that the Danes had the advantage of greater numbers, and they broke through the English shield-wall. Many of the English fled, but Byrhtnoth's own bodyguard closed around him and fought to the very end, lying dead in heaps around the body of their fallen leader.

There we have the English fighting spirit at its best. We recognise the same high morale that William of Malmesbury noted in his account of the English soldiery in the time of Edward the Elder and Athelstan (see page 111). In this episode at Maldon they were, of course, too sure of themselves, but theirs was not the attitude which loses wars.

In the days of Edward, Athelstan or the other warrior kings, the Essex contingent would have been backed up by adequate reserves, led by the king himself. They would have been on those Danes before they had recovered from their efforts and would have made them sorry they ever landed in England. But Ethelred held a conference and decided to offer the Danes a tribute to stay away. There lay the difference.

One other interesting point emerges from the story. *The Chronicle* states specifically, in two separate entries, that the advice to make peace with the Danish leader and to offer a tribute came from Archbishop Siric, who had succeeded Dunstan. One imagines that Dunstan's reaction would have been far different. Ethelred's commonly applied *sobriquet*, 'The Unready' is a mistaken reading for 'The Redeless', which means 'lacking in good counsel'. We can perhaps read in it a criticism of Archbishop Siric and other advisers on whom Ethelred relied.

Ethelred had other problems. He had to deal with cowards and traitors.

Having paid the Danes their protection money he called a council-meeting at London and decided that 'all the ships that were of any account should be gathered together at London.' The land-forces were also apparently reorganised, the command being given to two bishops and two aldermen, one of whom was Alderman Elfric of Mercia. Their orders were to try to entrap the enemy. But treachery was at work:

Then sent Alderman Elfric and gave warning to the enemy; and on the night preceding the day of battle he skulked away from the army, to his great disgrace. The enemy then escaped, except the crew of one ship, who were slain on the spot.

The details of the campaign are confused, but it is clear that the English got the worst of it and lost some of their ships.

This was in 992, but 11 years later Alderman Elfric was still in a position of authority, for the entry in *The Anglo-Saxon Chronicle* for 1003 reports scathingly:

In the same year came the army up into Wiltshire. Then was collected a very great force, from Wiltshire and from Hampshire; which was soon ready in their march upon the enemy; and Alderman Elfric should have led them on; but he brought forth his old tricks, and as soon as they were so near, that either army looked on the other, then he pretended sickness and began to retch, saying he was sick; and so betrayed the people that he should have led.

So the English army retreated, and Sweyn, the Danish king, carried on with his work of devastation and sacked Wilton.

Another incident in this deplorable reign illustrates how deeply the rot had set in. The account in *The Anglo-Saxon Chronicle* is by the hand of a contemporary writer, who reveals by his phraseology that the events are occurring as he records them. He is able to provide graphic details. In the year 1008 Ethelred decreed that a new fleet should be built, quickly. Every landowner possessing 310 hides of land (a hide being probably reckoned as sufficient to support a peasant family for a year) had to provide 'one galley or skiff'. Every man who owned eight hides had to supply a helmet and breastplate. All the ships and armour were ready in the following year,

And there were so many of them as never were in England before, in any king's days, as books tell us. And they were all transported together to Sandwich; that they should lie there and defend this land against any out-force.

But the great armament was dissipated and achieved nothing. One of the leading thanes, a man named Brihtric, 'betrayed Wulnoth, the South-Saxon knight, to the king'. Wulnoth, driven into exile, managed to persuade the captains of 20 of the ships to accompany him. They sailed along the south coast of England, plundering as they went. Presently news came to Brihtric that Wulnoth had moved into a position where he could easily be caught at a disadvantage. So Brihtric put out from Sandwich with 80 ships, eager to seize Wulnoth 'and acquire for himself much reputation'. Unfortunately a great gale blew up 'which beat and tossed the ships and drove them aground', whereupon Wulnoth's little fleet came up and burned them all. That was bad enough, but in the eyes of the chronicler the king's reaction was even worse:

When this was known to the remaining ships, where the king was . . . it was then as if all were lost. The king went home, with the aldermen and the nobility; and thus lightly did they forsake the ships; whilst the men that were in them rowed them back to London. Thus lightly did they suffer the labour of all the people to be in vain; nor was the terror lessened, as all England hoped.

What a contrast with Alfred's reaction to a much worse disaster.

Further events of that same year show the same pattern of defeatism. As soon as the fleet had moved out of Sandwich, a large army of Danes moved in and marched towards Canterbury. The men of east Kent then made a separate peace with them, paying a protection fee of 3,000 pounds. Central government had manifestly broken down; it was necessary for each district to make the best terms it could. And, again in the same year, the same army came around to the Isle of Wight and sent plundering expeditions into the heart of Sussex, Hampshire and even into Berkshire,

Then ordered the king to summon out all the population, that men might hold firm against them on every side; but nevertheless they marched as they pleased. On one occasion the king had begun his march before them, as they proceeded to their ships, and all the people were ready to fall upon them; but the plan was frustrated through Alderman Edric, as it ever is still.

By describing these events of the year 1009 we have moved ahead of our story and, indeed, there is little point in supplying a detailed account of the catalogue of disasters that comprised Ethelred's reign. With every failure on the part of the English, the Danish raids increased and intensified. In 994 they were led by Olaf Tryggvason, the king of Norway, and Sweyn, then crown prince of Denmark. On this occasion Ethelred bought peace by the payment of 16,000 pounds.

From 997 to the end of the century the Viking armies did not apparently go home at the end of the campaigning season but remained either in England or on the other side of the Channel, in Normandy. When, in the year 999, they were over-running Kent, the scribe who wrote *The Anglo-Saxon Chronicle* comments in exasperation:

The king with his council determined to proceed against them with sea and land forces; but as soon as the ships were ready, then arose delay from day to day, which harassed the miserable crews that lay on board; so that, always, the forwarder it should have been, the later it was. . . . Thus, in the end, these expeditions both by sea and land served no other purpose but to vex the people, to waste their treasure and to strengthen their enemies.

Impotent as the feckless Ethelred was against the Danes, however, he could do his own share of devastation and plundering when he had the chance, for when in the summer of the year 1000 the Vikings moved over to Normandy he used the respite to invade Strathclyde. He 'laid waste nearly the whole of it with his army', while his fleet did the same work of destruction in Anglesey.

In 1001 the Danish fleet was back from Normandy, pillaging first Devonshire and then Hampshire. Again peace was bought, this time for a tribute of 24,000 pounds. The wealth that England had accumulated during the reigns of the previous competent monarchs is perhaps best demonstrated by these frequent colossal tributes which the country was able to find, in addition to all the treasure to which the Danes helped themselves.

The end of the year 1002 was marked by the massacre of St. Brice's Day—13 November—when Ethelred ordered all the Danes resident in England to be killed. To have carried out the order in its entirety would have been impossible, for the greater part of the population in the north-eastern half of England was either Danish or half-bred, but it was certainly obeyed in many parts of the kingdom, including London. Among the victims was a hostage, Gunhilda, sister of Sweyn, now king of Denmark. She was said to have been a lady of considerable beauty who, before being beheaded, saw her husband murdered and her young son transfixed by four spears. The massacre was long remembered and served no purpose except to rouse the Danes who were safely out of the country to bitter hostility. It was a cowardly act, typical of a frustrated king uncertain of himself and unable to achieve anything else.

The direct consequence of Ethelred's crime was a series of massive invasions by the Danes, led now by Sweyn, who as king of Denmark controlled much of Norway and southern Sweden as well as his own country. They were in England in 1003, 1004 and early 1005. Withdrawing in the summer of 1005, they were back again in the following year. In another futile gesture Ethelred

ordered out all the population from Wessex and from Mercia; and they lay out all the harves under arms against the enemy; but it availed nothing more than it had often done before. . . . The enemy went wheresoever they would; they harrowed and burned down and slew as they went.

Meanwhile the harvest lay spoiling while the men who should have gathered it waited in vain for a chance to get at the robbers. In the autumn the marauding Danes made a rendezvous at Kennet, in north Wiltshire, easily beat off an English detachment which attacked them, and marched south to join their ships in Southampton Water. . . .

There might the people of Winchester see the rank and iniquitous foe, as they passed by their gates to the sea, fetching their meat and plunder over an extent of fifty miles from the sea.

Ethelred retreated to spend the winter in the un-devastated county of Shropshire, where he and his council decided to pay off the Danes yet again. This time the bribe was 30,000 pounds.

Well might the chronicler comment bitterly, 'They would not offer tribute in time, or fight with them; but when they had done most mischief, then they entered into peace and amity with them.'

In 1009 occurred the episodes relating to the new fleet and its partial destruction, already related. 1010 saw the Danes harrying in East Anglia, where they encountered resistance from an English leader of the old school, Ulfcytel, though he could not prevent them from raiding far into Mercia. In 1011 the main Danish army appeared in Kent and laid siege to Canterbury. An abbot named Elfmar let them in by treachery and was allowed to go unharmed, but the Archbishop, Alfeah (or Alphege), they took as a hostage, for ransom. The enormous sum they demanded, as protection-money for Kent, 48,000 pounds, could not be raised until the following year, 1012. Even then they would not let the Archbishop go but demanded a separate ransom for him. The heroic Archbishop would not only not promise them anything but forbade anyone to try to raise ransom money for him, whereupon the Danes killed him. Drunk with imported wine, a gang of them 'overwhelmed him with bones and horns of oxen; and one of them smote him with an axe-iron on the head, so that he sunk downwards with the blow.' Thus another saint was created.

Next year, 1013, Sweyn of Denmark arrived in the north with the intention of making himself king of England. He had a large fleet and army and rightly calculated that the Danes of the eastern and northern counties would not be averse from accepting him as their ruler. Within a few months he had secured control of almost the whole country—even at last, at the end of the year—of London. Ethelred fled to Normandy, 'And all the people fully received Sweyn and considered him full king.'

Early in 1014 Sweyn died and the situation changed drastically. Canute, his son and successor, was a young man so far untried in war and uncertain of what was happening back home in Denmark. Until Easter Canute remained at the Danish headquarters at Gainsborough, and meantime Ethelred, advised that the coast was clear, returned to London, where he was received with more enthusiasm than he deserved. Canute set about raising a local army in the North, particularly in Lindsey, but Ethelred brought up his army before Canute was ready, and the latter had little alternative but to take to his ships. He sailed away down the coast to Kent, leaving his unfortunate allies in Lindsey to the mercy of Ethelred, who punished them ruthlessly, for he could be merciless when encountering little or no opposition. With Canute, who had landed at Sandwich, he parleyed, buying him off eventually with more 'Danegeld'—21,000 pounds.

Canute, having returned to Denmark and settled affairs, being on good terms with his elder brother Harold who had become king there, returned to England in the late summer of 1015. This was to be his kingdom. Landing in Wessex, he fought an indecisive campaign, being opposed belatedly by a true heir of the House of Egbert, Edmund Ironside, of whom we read in the next chapter. The war was still in progress, with an assault on London imminent, when on 23 April king Ethelred died.

Unlike so many of his predecessors he had had a long reign, 38 years. It had been a period of unmitigated catastrophe; from a peak of unsurpassed prosperity in the time of king Edgar England had sunk into a state of chaotic misery. The common people and many of the lesser nobility retained their old sterling qualities, but with an ineffectual king at the rudder the ship of state drifted aimlessly. Treachery and duplicity flourished; no man knew whom he could trust. William of Malmesbury, assessing the king's character from the vantage-point of a hundred or so years, comments,

The king, admirably calculated for sleeping, did nothing but postpone and hesitate, and if ever he recovered his senses enough to raise himself upon his elbow, he quickly relapsed into his original wretchedness. . . . His brother's ghost also tormented him. Who can tell how often he collected his army? how often he ordered ships to be built? how frequently he called out commanders from all quarters? and yet nothing was ever effected.

In appearance Ethelred is said to have been taller than average, fair-haired and handsome. He liked soft living and spent much time in drinking, feasting and sharing the beds of a whole series of women.

Even the redoubtable Edmund was his son by an obscure woman whose name is not recorded.

XIV

Edmund Ironside

Edmund Ironside, the eldest son of Ethelred of whom we have any record, appears on the scene in the summer of 1015. Nothing is known of his life before that time. He comes on the stage as a young man 'of great strength both of mind and person', says William of Malmesbury. Any personable young prince of that type must have seemed like a god to the tormented English, who soon gave him the nickname 'Ironside'.

His first act was not altogether promising, being a domestic intrigue. Early in 1015 at a great council at Oxford Alderman Edric Streona of Mercia, a treacherous and self-seeking character, murdered two senior thanes from the east of the country.

Although the king is not said to have been involved in the crime, he evidently sided with Edric, for he sequestrated the possessions of the two noblemen and had the widow of one of them, Sigfirth, incarcerated in the abbey at Malmesbury. Hearing about this, Edmund went over to Malmesbury to see the lady and, finding her beautiful, married her. Then, without officially informing his father, he went back to the Danelaw, east of Watling Street, and claimed for himself the property of the two murdered thanes. After a few depredations to show that he meant business, Edmund was accepted as king by the Five Towns (Derby, Leicester, Lincoln, Nottingham and Stamford) and by all the surrounding countryside. Evidently he was especially welcome in Lindsey, still smarting under the evil treatment meted out by both Ethelred and Canute.

About the same time Canute came back from Denmark, to claim what he confidently expected would be his kingdom. He landed first of all in Kent, then went on to Wessex where his army started to plunder. Hearing of this, Edmund began to collect an army in the North to oppose him; Alderman Edric started to do the same in Mercia. Meanwhile, the unhappy Ethelred was lying ill at Corsham, in north Wiltshire. Edmund and Edric joined forces but Edric, devious as ever, evidently had plans to desert to Canute and betray Edmund. This Edmund learned of in time and moved his army away from Edric's. Edric thereupon 'seduced' 40 ships from the king and handed them over to Canute.

The winter wore on. The people of Wessex had submitted to Canute and agreed to provide horses for his army. The king was still sick. Before spring came, Canute and Edric together raided into the heart of Mercia, penetrating from the upper Thames as far as Warwickshire 'and plundered therein and burned, and slew all they met'—a shocking crime for a Mercian earl in his own territory.

Twice during the winter and spring months Edmund Ironside raised an army, only to see it melt away before it could be used. The problem was that, even now, the soldiers considered that their allegiance was to the king. They demanded that Ethelred should come and lead them or, at least, show himself as their leader. But Ethelred had got to the stage when he was suspicious of everyone. He abandoned all who were trying to help him and retreated to London. Edmund then went north to try to assemble an army there. Uhtred, the earl of Northumbria, offered to help, but when they joined forces Edmund soon found himself helping to harry and plunder in Shropshire and Staffordshire instead of opposing the main enemy. Canute, predictably, marched his Danish army up the Fosse Way and so towards York. Uhtred, alarmed, broke off his pillaging expedition and went over to meet him. Out of necessity, says *The Chronicle*, he offered his submission, which was accepted. But soon afterwards the false Edric persuaded Canute to have him murdered.

With such troops as he had of his own Edmund, while all this was happening, marched across country and joined his father in London. There he was when Ethelred died, on 23 April 1016. In the meantime Canute had returned to Wessex and was with his fleet at Southampton. As soon as the news of Ethelred's death was known, two rival kings were appointed. The Londoners and as many noblemen and ecclesiastics as were in London unanimously accepted Edmund. The leaders of the rest of the country, probably more numerous and influential than those in London, met at Southampton and offered Canute their allegiance if he would consent to govern justly and according to their laws. Canute agreed.

The rival armies now changed places. Edmund advanced into Wessex and seems to have been successful in occupying most of it. While he was thus engaged, Canute sailed his fleet around to the Thames and invested London. Both had plenty of time for their operations, as neither was engaged by the main forces of the other. Edmund, either at this stage or later, in June, fought at least two battles, one at Penselwood (in Somerset) and one at Sherston (in north Wiltshire). Canute moved his fleet up to London Bridge; then, finding that it blocked his way upstream, he had a channel cut to by-pass the bridge and the city along the southern side. When it was complete he took a part of his fleet through this canal to the upper river, thus cutting off the city from reinforcements and supplies from the landward side. He threw up earthworks to encompass the walls and prepared for a siege.

Leaving his men to keep the Londoners shut in, Canute then took part of his army down to Wessex to try conclusions with Edmund there. It is on this occasion that the battles of Penselwood and Sherston may have occurred. Nothing decisive resulted, however, and the two kings seem to have returned to London by different routes, Canute to continue the siege, Edmund to relieve the city. This time there was considerable fighting. Edmund, evidently a good general, took his army by unfrequented ways north of the Thames and so attacked the Danes from an unexpected quarter. He succeeded in driving them from their trenches and sent them flying to their ships, but he and his army could not then follow them because there was no ford across the river nearer than Brentford, some miles upstream. By the time Edmund had assembled his forces there and had got across the Danes had had time to improve their defences south of the Thames. A second great battle ensued, in which the English again claimed the victory, but their losses were so heavy—due, says *The Chronicle*, to their own impetuosity—that Edmund had to retire to Wessex to raise reinforcements.

With Edmund out of the way, Canute tried a direct assault on the city but according to *The Chronicle*, 'almighty God delivered them'. The citizens of London had on more than one occasion, since Alfred had fortified their city, shown themselves to be a formidable fighting force. Thwarted there, and probably running short of provisions, Canute abandoned the siege and sailed downstream to Essex. Anchoring in the mouth of the Orwell he dispatched a plundering expedition into the heart of Mercia, apparently to replenish supplies, for meat is specifically mentioned in their loot. Then, their ships provisioned, the Danes sailed south again and landed at the mouth of the Medway. Before they had settled down, Edmund with an English army was at their throats. In a violent battle at Otford he soundly defeated them, thus showing what a more energetic leader than Ethelred might have done years before. The Danes fled in haste to the Isle of Sheppey, the English following and slaughtering the stragglers.

With the ambition, like the Vicar of Bray, to be always on the winning side, the alarmed Alderman Edric again played the turncoat. Immediately after the battle of Otford he came to Edmund's camp and offered his allegiance. The writer of *The Anglo-Saxon Chronicle* comments that in accepting it Edmund could not have been more ill-advised.

By autumn supplies were running short again in Canute's camp, so the Danes moved over again to Essex and started another raid into Mercia. When he learned what was happening, Edmund moved across the Thames with his army and advanced into Essex. There he met the Danes, who were returning from their Midland foray, at Ashingdon, on a slight elevation of land between the Thames and the Crouch estuaries. No sooner was the battle joined than Alderman Edric, the arch-traitor, withdrew, taking his soldiers with him. With his flank thus exposed and a sizeable part of his forces gone, Edmund had little chance. His men fought valiantly but in the end were completely defeated. Half the nobility of England lay slain and Edmund himself, like Alfred so many years earlier, became a fugitive.

Fleeing westwards, he came to the Severn in Gloucestershire, with Canute in pursuit. Meanwhile, to judge from the wording of *The Anglo-Saxon Chronicle*, Edric had gone over to Canute, as perhaps he had planned from the first, and was acting as a counsellor. His advice was to make peace with Edmund, and Canute, recognising a formidable opponent of far different calibre than Ethelred, thought it good. The two kings met at Deerhurst, on the Severn bank, and signed a treaty whereby they divided England between them: the boundary was to be the Thames. Edmund was to be king of everything south of the river; Canute of all land to the north. Edmund thus took Wessex, and Canute the rest of England.

The arrangement bears all the hallmarks of an interim agreement. It would not have lasted. Edmund in particular was not in favour of any accommodation and, instead, proposed a duel between himself and Canute —winner take all. Canute, taking stock of his rival's considerable and muscular bulk compared with his own rather diminutive size, declined. Edmund then allowed himself to be persuaded to agree to the treaty, but indubitably both sides would have been watching the other, looking for an opportunity to gain the maximum advantage by breaking it. When the formalities had been concluded the Danes returned to London, with which city they concluded a separate treaty, requiring it to pay a substantial indemnity. And at London they settled down for the winter. On 30 November, however, Edmund Ironside died. Realising that now they had little option, the West Saxon council elected Canute as their king.

The death of Edmund Ironside was altogether too convenient to be accepted as natural. A big, burly man, he seems to have been in excellent health during the meeting at Deerhurst. A hundred years later rumours were still circulating, and William of Malmesbury passes on some that he heard. All place the responsibility on the traitor Edric, who is said to have ordered his servants to commit the murder. According to William, Canute, who learned about the circumstances through the murderers approaching him for an expected reward, at first pretended to be satisfied. Then he brought the guilty men before an assembly of some of his chief counsellors and invited them to tell just how the deed was done. The assassins, anticipating that this was the prelude to their reward, regaled the company with the details, whereupon the king ordered them out to immediate execution.

As for Edric, at the very first Canute divided his kingdom into four parts, he himself taking direct charge of Wessex, while Edric had control of Mercia and two other earls of the other sections. Edric thus received for his double-dealing the payment which he coveted. But he over-reached himself. Not long afterwards, according to William, during a heated argument he reproached Canute with the words, 'I first deserted Edmund for your sake, and afterwards even despatched him in consequence of my engagements to you.' At this the king became very angry. 'Thou shalt die, and justly,' he decreed,

since thou art guilty of treason both to God and to me, by having killed thy own sovereign and my sworn brother. Thy blood be upon thine own head, because thy mouth hath spoken against thee, and thou hast lifted thy hand against the Lord's Anointed.

Immediately, says William, Edric was strangled there in the room where they sat and his body thrown out of the window into the Thames. It was a sensible though ruthless move on Canute's part. As Edric had betrayed one king, so he might betray another when the opportunity offered; and anyway he had outlived his usefulness as far as Canute was concerned.

So, in the end, the Danes triumphed and a Danish king reigned over England. It is true that, in spite of the bloodthirsty track he hewed in making his way to the throne, he proved to be a good king, doing much to reconcile the two races over which he ruled. Above all, for 18 years he gave peace to the stricken and exhausted land. He married Emma, the widow of king Ethelred, who seems much to have preferred him to her first husband. His government was firm but just; in his breadth of vision he resembled, to some extent, Alfred.

The Anglo-Saxon Chronicle entry for the year 1029 consists of one sentence only: 'This year King Canute returned home to England.' Home. England, not Denmark, was his home, as it was for tens of thousands of both Englishmen and Danes. Out of the warring elements a united nation was being fashioned.

But tribute must be paid to that lion-like man, Edmund Ironside. If only a generation could have been skipped, so that he succeeded the martyred Edward, how different things might have been in England, and what miseries the people might have escaped. He stands, worthy of his great ancestors, the last Warrior King of the House of Wessex.

XV

Epilogue

The domestic life of Canute and Emma seems to have been especially harmonious, despite the facts that the marriage was in the first place a political one and that Emma was ten years older than her husband. Among the matters on which they were apparently agreed was that Canute's successor to the throne should be their son, Harthacnut. Unfortunately for this arrangement Canute, in common with most men who succumb before the age of eighty, died before he had expected to.

His death occurred at Shaftesbury on 12 November, 1035. He was aged about forty-six and had reigned over England for nearly 20 years. If Harthacnut had been on the spot he could have taken over with few questions asked, but at the crucial moment he was in Denmark. And there he had to stay, keeping an eye on Norway where a new king, Magnus, was threatening to avenge ancient wrongs that his people had suffered at Danish hands. An absentee monarch was the last thing that England needed, so the council of state met to exercise its ancient prerogative of choosing a king from the royal family. After much opposition from the Wessex contingent they elected Harold, a half-brother of Harthacnut. His mother is said to have been Elfgivu, a lady of Northampton who, although she was apparently not legally married to Canute, was recognised as a royal wife by many nobles and prelates and who exercised considerable authority in the North. One of Harold's first acts was to raid the royal treasury at Winchester, which had been left in Queen Emma's custody. Queen Emma herself thought it wise to depart to her brother's court in Flanders, though *The Anglo-Saxon Chronicle* says that she was 'driven out, without any pity, against the raging winter'.

The negotiations that resulted in Harold's election took the best part of two years. In that interregnum, while Emma was still at Winchester, one of her sons by her first husband, King Ethelred, came over from Normandy to visit her. His name was Alfred. Whether he genuinely wanted to see his mother or whether, as seems more likely, he saw a chance of fishing in troubled waters, is not known, but he chose an unfortunate moment. Negotiations concerning Harold were at a delicate stage, and the presence of Alfred was an unwanted complication. He was seized, held for a time and then so clumsily blinded that he died soon afterwards. William of Malmesbury recounts that of Alfred's followers one man out of ten, chosen by lot, was saved and the rest beheaded.

The person popularly accused of the crime was Earl Godwin, of Wessex, a man rising to great power. His version was that, although he arrested Alfred for his own safety, the prince was afterwards kidnapped out of his keeping. Godwin had to stand trial before the great council of the kingdom but had a sufficient number of peers to support him to avoid trouble. Rumour accused Queen Emma, too, of being implicated in the murder of her own son. She vigorously denied the charge, offering to submit to the ordeal of walking over red-hot plough-shares in Winchester Cathedral to prove her innocence. Some accounts read as though she actually underwent the ordeal, but that is doubtful.

After a reign of four years Harold died of an illness. Harthacnut, who had by now settled his affairs in Denmark and was on his way with a fleet to claim the English throne, stepped into his shoes without dispute. On the way he called in at Bruges, in Flanders, to see his mother and spent some time there, perhaps waiting for Harold's death.

Harthacnut reigned for just short of two years. He died during a drinking bout. He made himself unpopular by insisting that the English pay the wages of the crews of the 62 ships he brought over with him, a transaction which involved the handing over of more than 32,000 pounds, which the English regarded as yet more Danegeld. He also dug up the corpse of his half-brother Harold and had it beheaded and thrown into the Thames. On the other hand, he received his other half-brother Edward at his court and treated him amicably.

This Edward, on the death of Harthacnut, was accepted as king without question. He was, after all, pure English, being the son of Emma and Ethelred the Redeless and so younger brother to the murdered Alfred. And the Danish nobles apparently took their cue from Harthacnut, who seems to have regarded Edward as at any rate a potential successor of whom he approved. The situation is obscure, however, for Queen Emma seems absent from the list of Edward's supporters, and there was no love lost between him and his mother. One of his first acts was to confiscate all her vast treasure and properties, though he allowed her to live at Winchester to the end of her days. With Edward the royal house of Wessex returns to the English throne. The character of Edward, popularly known as 'The Confessor', is an enigma. He was undoubtedly an exceptionally religious man and even an ascetic. He was patient, peaceable and popularly regarded as a saint. Certainly he cannot be classified as a Warrior King. But then, he had no-one to fight.

The Danish wars were over. After the death of Harthacnut it was tacitly agreed that England and Denmark should become separate kingdoms. On the other hand, England was now half-Danish. Danes and people of mixed Danish and English descent were predominant in the northern and eastern parts of the country; the court which Edward took over had a preponderance of Danish nobles. And Edward himself, though English by birth, had lived in exile in Normandy for so long that he had little direct knowledge of English ways and English people. Some of those with whom he now had to co-operate, and in particular the Wessex Earl Godwin, he liked even less than the rough Danes.

Thus isolated, a peace-loving monarch in what was to him a kingdom of aliens, there was little he could do but exercise tact and patience. This he did with such consummate skill that he died, presumably of old age, in 1066, after a reign of 24 years, respected, even revered, and mourned by the whole nation. When he felt himself strong enough, politically, he acted with decisive energy in banishing Earl Godwin and all his brood. When the situation was reversed and he could no longer challenge the Earl, he accepted the situation philosophically and arrived at an agreement with him. So ascetic in his habits that he was widely supposed to be celibate, he perhaps derived a wry satisfaction from depriving Godwin, whose daughter he married, of the pleasure of becoming the grandfather of the next English king. Quite possibly he favoured William of Normandy as his heir as a means of settling a few old scores with the house of Godwin, though Normandy, where he had spent his long exile and which was rapid changing through the absorption of French civilisation, was his spiritual home.

We can probably see in Edward (he should rightly be Edward III of England) the counterpart of his pious ancestor Ethelwulf. Some features of his character bear a notable resemblance to those of Alfred. He loved books and learning, and the church which, of course, assured him good publicity at the hands of monastic chroniclers. All in all, he was not an unworthy descendant of the warrior kings.

Edward died on 5 January of the fateful year 1066. The direct heir to the throne was Edgar, son of his brother Alfred, but he was only a child and the times demanded a man at the helm. At a council in London Harold, the son of Earl Godwin, was chosen as king, largely because he seemed to be the only man capable of governing the kingdom and meeting the external dangers which threatened.

Harold reigned for only nine months, which were filled with wars and alarms. In the previous year his younger brother Tostig had been sent into exile. Inept government in Northumbria, of which he was earl, led to a successful revolt there. In the political settlement which followed, the banishment of Tostig was one of the prices which King Edward had had to pay for peace in the North. Tostig went off to Flanders and planned mischief.

When in the spring of 1066 he appeared off the south coast with a fleet and started plundering, Harold thought he had been put up to it by William of Normandy, who had been making no secret of his claim to the English throne. He marched an army down to Sandwich, where Tostig had landed. Immediately he was up against that problem of the defence of Britain which had bedevilled all the English kings since the Danish menace first began—namely, the difficulty of protecting a long coastline against an enemy who had command of the sea. No sooner had Harold arrived at Sandwich than Tostig moved along the coast to Norfolk. Pursued there, he progressed to Lindsey where, however, he was caught by Earl Edwin of Mercia and defeated in a pitched battle. On this, many of his ships deserted, and Tostig went on to take refuge in Scotland with only about a dozen of them.

All that summer the Norman menace grew. Harold called out the southern militia and had them stand to arms right through the summer months. At the same time, a formidable English fleet patrolled the English Channel, ready for action. But the long months of waiting proved irksome, and the harvest was ungathered. In the second week of September Harold disbanded the militia and brought the fleet back to anchor in the Thames.

At this juncture, quite unexpectedly, a Norwegian fleet commanded by the king of Norway, Harold Hardrada, and accompanied by the renegade Tostig, arrived off Northumbria. All the ships that could be spared having been sent south to watch events in Normandy, the Norwegians landed unopposed from the Yorkshire Ouse and advanced on York. They were met by the northern and midland Earls, Edwin and Morcar, who gave them a fiercely-contested battle near the village of Gate Fulford, but the Norwegian army was too strong, and the English were driven back with the loss of many men.

On 24 September, four days after this battle, Harold arrived at York. Passing through it, he encountered the invading army at Stamford Bridge and there inflicted on them one of the great defeats of English history. Harold Hardrada, a giant of a man and one of the greatest generals of the age, was slain, as was Earl Tostig, and the Norwegian army became a rabble of fugitives. It was a remarkable achievement by an English army which had just completed a forced march from London, though the

Norwegian forces may have been considerably weakened by heavy losses at Gate Fulford.

Only three days later the wind changed and allowed William of Normandy's fleet, which had been waiting in its ports for so long, to cross the Channel and land in Pevensey Bay. The English fleet was still laid up in the Thames. Once on land, however, William was in no hurry to move. He had no idea as to the size of the army which would in due course oppose him nor, indeed, whether its leader would be Harold of Wessex or Harold Hardrada and his Norwegians. So he waited within easy reach of his ships should the need arise for him to retreat back to Normandy. Harold, on hearing the news, hastily made a settlement in the North and hurried south again. The tremendous marches by which he took his army 200 miles to Yorkshire and then 200 miles back to London in such a short time have excited the admiration of historians and military experts ever since. No-one could have been more vigorous or have acted more quickly.

In the end, Harold's very energy proved his undoing. Arrived back in London, he should have awaited the arrival of the forces which he had summoned from all parts of the country. He might then have been able to meet William with overwhelming strength. As it was, he pushed on into Sussex with his tried army who had accompanied him to Yorkshire and with few others. He met William on 14 October in a great fight known afterwards as the Battle of Hastings and, after a contest in which the issue hung for long in the balance, was eventually slain. His personal bodyguard died in heaps around his standard.

If ever a king had cause to complain that the Fates were unfair to him, it was Harold. He had been called upon to fight two major battles almost simultaneously at either end of his kingdom, and he only just failed. The first of the two was an overwhelming victory in which he defeated one of the most celebrated warriors of his time; the second came near to success. Having conceded this, we must admit that Harold was outmatched in generalship. Not only would a wiser general have waited till he had his optimum force, but his ideas of the use of men in battle were obsolete. He still relied on the old grouping of warriors on foot behind a shield-wall, whereas William, who had learned warfare in a more progressive school on the Continent, employed his troops in an altogether more versatile fashion. He used mounted knights, fighting from horseback; and his archers formed an important corps which lent planned and controlled support to the other divisions.

So Harold fell, and with him the curtain descended on Saxon England. Though not of the royal blood of the old House of Wessex, he carried on nobly the traditions of the Warrior Kings.

The House of Wessex

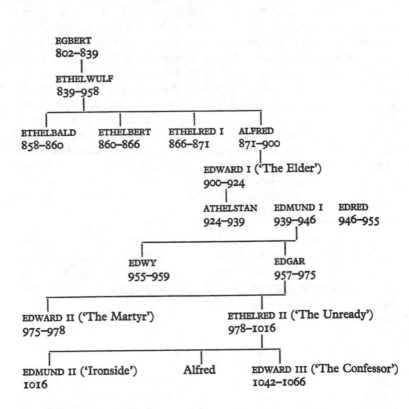

EGBERT
802–839

ETHELWULF
839–958

ETHELBALD   ETHELBERT   ETHELRED I   ALFRED
858–860   860–866   866–871   871–900

EDWARD I ('The Elder')
900–924

ATHELSTAN   EDMUND I   EDRED
924–939   939–946   946–955

EDWY   EDGAR
955–959   957–975

EDWARD II ('The Martyr')   ETHELRED II ('The Unready')
975–978   978–1016

EDMUND II ('Ironside')   Alfred   EDWARD III ('The Confessor')
1016   1042–1066

Note: The gap from 1016 to 1042 was occupied by the Danish kings, CANUTE (1016–1035), HAROLD I (1035–40) and HARTHACNUT (1040–1043). HAROLD II (1066) was loosely connected to the House of Wessex by the marriage of his sister Edith to EDWARD III, 'The Confessor'.

BIBLIOGRAPHY

ALCOCK, LESLIE   *Arthur's Britain*, 1971
Anglo-Saxon Chronicle
Annales Cambriae
ARBMAN, H.   *The Vikings*, 1961
ASHE, GEOFFREY   *King Arthur's Avalon*, 1957
   From Caesar to Arthur, 1960
   Land to the West, 1962
   (ed.)   *The Quest for Arthur's Britain*, 1971
ASSER   *Annals of the Deeds of Alfred the Great*
BARBER, RICHARD   *The Figure of Arthur*, 1972
BEDE   *Ecclesiastical History of the English People*, ed. V. Scudder, 1954
BLAIR, P. H.   *An Introduction to Anglo-Saxon England*, 1956
BRØNSTED, JOHANNES   *The Vikings*, 1960
BRUCE-MITFORD, R. L. S. ed.   *Recent Archaeological Excavations in Britain*, 1956
CHADWICK, H. M.   *The Origin of the English Nation*, 1907
   The Heroic Age, 1912
CHADWICK, NORA   *Celtic Britain*, 1963
CHAMBERS, R. W.   *England before the Norman Conquest*, 1926
   Beowulf, 1932
CHURCHILL, SIR WINSTON   *A History of the English-Speaking Peoples* Vol. I, 1956
COLLINGWOOD, R. G. AND MYRES, J. N. L.   *Roman Britain and the English Settlements*, 1937
COPLEY, G. J.   *The Conquest of Wessex in the Sixth Century*, 1954
DUCKETT, E. S.   *Anglo-Saxon Saints and Scholars*, 1947
De Excidio et Conquestu Britanniae (attributed to Gildas)
HARDEN, D. B.   *Dark Age Britain*, 1956
HANNING, R. W.   *The Vision of History in Early Britain*, 1966
HODGKIN, R. G.   *A History of the Anglo-Saxons*, 1952
HOVGAARD, W.   *The Voyages of the Norsemen to America*, 1914
KENDRICK, T. D.   *A History of the Vikings*, 1930
LLOYD, J. E.   *History of Wales*, 1911
NENNIUS   *History of the Britons* (ed. A. W. Wade-Evans), 1938
OMAN, SIR C.   *England before the Norman Conquest*, 1938
PAULL, P.   *The Life of Alfred the Great*, 1884
RICHMOND, I. A.   *Roman Britain*, 1955
STENTON, SIR F.   *Anglo-Saxon England*, 1947.
TREVELYAN, G. M.   *History of England*, 1945
TURVILLE-PETRE, G.   *The Heroic Age of Scandinavia*, 1951
VINOGRADOFF, P. *English Society in the 11th Century*, 1908
WHITELOCKE, D.   *Anglo-Saxon Wills*, 1930
WHITLOCK, R.   *Somerset*, 1975
   Wiltshire, 1976
WILLIAM OF MALMESBURY   *Chronicle of the Kings of England*, ed. 1847
WILSON, D.   *The Anglo-Saxons*, 1960 (revised ed. 1971)

Index